Feminism
BACKWARDS

Feminism
BACKWARDS

ROSITA SWEETMAN

MERCIER PRESS

MERCIER PRESS

Cork

www.mercierpress.ie

ISBN: 978 1 78117 749 5

A CIP record for this title is available from the British Library.

Printed and bound in the EU.

To my darling Chupi and Luke —
my sun, my moon and all my stars.

'The vote, I thought, means nothing to women,
we should be armed.'
Edna O'Brien, *Girls in their Married Bliss*, 1964

'I wasn't born a feminist. Life made me one.'
Mamo McDonald, ICA

'Each time a woman stands up for herself, without
knowing it, possibly without claiming it, she stands up
for all women.'
Maya Angelou

'Feminism, in its true sense, is no more than the attempt to
restore to the human community part of its own dignity.'
Eavan Boland

CONTENTS

PROLOGUE

Oh Ireland, you mad, crazy, schizophrenic creature you!

One minute you're hopeless and ruined, a rain-saturated hag, a priest-ridden, drink-sodden curmudgeonly disaster fucked over for centuries by the British, latterly ruled by hatchet-faced Catholic nuns and priests in full drag, one killing the mammies and the babbies inside laundries, the others abusing the babbies behind the altar, in the confessional, on the summer 'holidays', all the while delivering po-faced diktats from pulpit and podium about 'chastity' and 'purity'.

Another minute, Ireland, you're cowed, cowardly, post-colonial, venal, hypocritical, two-faced, with a great big fat inferiority complex stuck on your shoulder. Your politicians, schooled by priests and nuns, don't need to be told what to do by the Church, they have it done before the bishops even get their croziers out. There is only one kind of misbehaviour – being found out. Everything else can be shoved under the carpet – including the women and the babbies.

Darling Ireland, only nine years ago you went through a bank bust so ferocious it's classified as one of the worst in banking history, with huge chunks of your beautiful, educated young having to emigrate; your builders, sons and grandsons of the builders of America, much of England, having to up sticks to Australia and Canada; many of your 'ordinary' people losing their life savings; with those unlucky enough to be on social welfare routinely abused, even blamed for the crash; with supports for the disabled, blind, sick and old cut to the bone, while the politicians and their banker buddies, who massaged the boom into the hideous bloated beast that it became, walked away with pensions of €3,000 a week! When the country was ruined! With one of the main banking players, who had jovially suggested to colleagues they pull a figure 'out of their arse' for the government regulators, getting a risible custodial sentence, and a mere three out of the other hundreds of boom boys, and girls, spending time in jail. Three!

Oh Ireland.

But before you could say 'Land of Saints and Scholars me arse', a fabulously beautiful new Ireland came into being on 25 May 2018, when 1.4 million people – many of them young emigrants flying home from Bangkok, Australia, London and Toronto, along with local women, men, grannies and grandads – voted to repeal the hideous Eighth Amendment to our constitution, freeing the way for the setting up of proper, safe and legal abortion services for our women here. At last.

One day we had faux priests and faux nuns, backed up by spineless politician chums, given apparently limitless time on the radio and TV, and in the newspapers, with money pouring in from America, to lecture us all good-o, threatening the usual fire and brimstone, eternal damnation in hell's hottest hole, etc., for any woman who even dared to think about whether she could or would or should not have a baby. Even if the baby was dying inside her with a fatal foetal abnormality? Yes, said the fire and brimstone ones. Even if she was fourteen, had been raped by her father, and was suicidal? Most definitely, said the fire and brimstoners. Even if she was just too tired, too young, too old, too poor, too scared, too unloved to bring another baby into this world? Absolutely, screamed the fire and brimstone ones. They should have their babies regardless; we'll get them adopted. Sure people are crying out for babbies to adopt.

As one writer, Donal O'Keefe, put it: 'The Eighth Amendment meant [a woman] wasn't dying enough to save her life until she was dying too much to save her life.'[1]

Yup, that's weird.

And then the people voted. And then the exit polls were taken. And, 'Landslide!' shouted *The Irish Times*, unable to bear the tension any longer, even though it was only an hour since the polls closed. 'Two-thirds majority in favour!' quoted RTÉ an hour later.

We were all astounded. We watched and waited all the next day as the counts took place, terrified some terrible mistake had been made, that it would be only the cities voting Yes, only the young people, only those returning home. But no. Right across the country, right across every age group,

---

1   *The Avondhu*, 16 May 2016.

every profession, every class, every sexuality, the two-thirds majority held.

YES, YES, YES, *YES*!

On the evening of the count there were jubilant scenes in the courtyard of Dublin Castle. The sun shone. The politicians were lauded. The campaigners, veterans and newbies were cheered to the rafters. A dog was held up like Simba in *The Lion King* and everyone went ballistic.

Next day some were a bit sniffy – imagine celebrating abortion, etc.; it's unseemly. But it wasn't the introduction of abortion that was being celebrated – it was the end of rule by Rome, by priests, by nuns, by fear, by hypocrisy, by that odious non-friend of humanity: respectability.

As journalist Fintan O'Toole said in a television discussion after the result, it was the end of an Ireland where we locked up women and children, where we *tortured* them, to maintain an illusion of piety.

It was a celebration for a new, hypocrisy-free Ireland where equality ruled. Where all the faux priests and nuns and preachers can preach away to their hearts' content but have no power to ram their doctrines into our laws. Into our constitution. Into our bodies.

Ailbhe Smyth, the seventy-plus-year-old activist in feminist and lesbian politics, and one of the heroines of the referendum, said it was the first time in her entire life that she felt fully free as a woman in this country; it was as if an enormous burden had been lifted – the burden of the puritanical past. Professor Mary Corcoran of Maynooth University said, on RTÉ's *Today with Seán O'Rourke* on 28 May 2018, that it was perhaps 'the final shift from a theocratic republic to a civic republic'.

On 25 May 2018 a new 'happy' and 'compassionate' Ireland was born; the old black-and-white and grey Ireland, the old hag, the old sow who ate her own farrow, was finally laid to rest as the work begun (again) by feminism reached a successful conclusion.

How far we had come!

ALL ABOARD

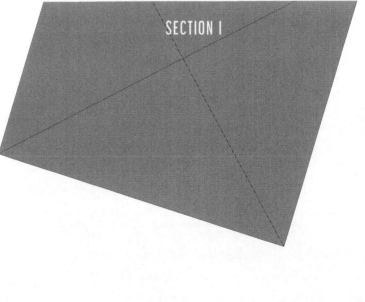

SECTION I

SO, WHO I?

I come from what was once a more or less functional big Catholic family in Dublin, Ireland. My mum and dad met on the steps of her mother's beautiful Georgian house, 24 Fitzwilliam Square, late one summer's evening when Mum opened the hall door to see her medical student brother – very, very drunk – being held up by a tall, skinny young barrister with very, very blue eyes. Dad said it was love at first sight. They began dating, but Mum told him that love would have to wait; she had a few things to do first.

Having left school, Mum had decided she wanted to become a nurse. Granny – or 'Gaga' as we (lovingly) called her after one of us mispronounced 'grandma' – who wouldn't even let her go 'downstairs' through the green baize door to the kitchens in Fitzwilliam Square to make a cup of tea, nearly lost her mind. There was NO WAY her daughter, whom she had spent years moulding into a 'lady', was going to become a nurse. No way! Nurses were skivvies! Nurses were nothing more than maids! Nurses were out of the question! There was a battle royale and, having lost the battle, Mum did what any young woman with self-respect would do – she left Gaga and Dad behind and headed up to Belfast, where she joined the war by signing on as an ambulance driver for the FANYs.

Take that, Mommie dearest.

She was there when the Nazis bombed seven kinds of hell out of Belfast in early May 1941: 900 people were killed, 1,500 seriously injured and, by some accounts, half of Belfast's housing stock was damaged or destroyed. Half of it.

Dad and Granny sat in the latter's drawing room, where Dad had been invited for afternoon tea. They listened to reports from the North on the radio, blank with terror.

Three days later a telegram arrived at Gaga's house. 'Alive and kicking, Una'.

Mum's finest hour.

Mum seems to have battled, had to battle, Gaga from the get-go. She was determined not to be her mother's plaything – a doll dressed in hand-stitched lawn-linen dresses with starched bonnets to match, photographed by the photographer of the day. *Non!* Mum wanted to be out riding with her brother, Denis; out with the other children who lived around the square; out with her adored dad, proudly holding the reins of his horse at a 'meet'. Her nickname was 'Punk'. Nothing and no one seemed to scare her.

Mum's father, a doctor with the British Army, then Master of the Coombe Lying-in Hospital in Dublin, had been killed out hunting when his horse rolled on top of him at a water ditch. He had adored Mum and she him. Aged fourteen, she had made the journey home from boarding school in England on the mailboat to find her father laid out on the dining-room table for an autopsy, Gaga white-haired with shock and out in the garden screaming at God for taking her beloved.

After Mum's return from Belfast, of course, all problems dissolved in the face of early married bliss. She and Dad set up home in 'Phoenix Hill', a beautiful Georgian house within the walls of the Phoenix Park; this was Grandfather and Granny Sweetman's wedding present to them. Their first baby was a boy – very important in those patriarchal days – and they were much in love. It was still during the war, or the 'Emergency' as we referred to it in Ireland. A time when huge drays brought carts stacked high with turf in from the mountain bogs, barefoot children from the slums running alongside to catch windfalls, with rationing on everything – butter, tea, eggs, not to mention nylon stockings. Still, Mum always seemed happy when she remembered those times: Dad just about to saw off the bannisters on the stairs to make a fire when a friend delivered a bucket of coal; Mum heading off on her bicycle, lamp dimmed for the blackout, to collect the butter and sugar Gaga had saved for her; Dad, in desperation, smoking cigarette butts stuck through with a pin, retrieved from the ashes of the grate.

Life was an adventure. Fun.

Then catastrophe struck. Dad contracted TB. In those days the barbaric treatment on offer involved sawing open the chest, collapsing the lungs – removing, in Dad's case, all of one lung and part of the second – followed by weeks lying on your back in a sanatorium. It was a disaster from which he never truly recovered.

Dad's ill health soon returned. By now they had four

children, and my twin sister and I were 'on the way'. Dad was packed off to a sanatorium in Switzerland again, 'Phoenix Hill' had to be sold and Mum had to go back and live in her mother's house.

She hated it. She raged against Dad for getting ill. It was his fault they'd been forced to sell their home, his fault she'd been forced, now with six children, back on her mother's hospitality. He was useless.

Of course it was unfair of Mum to blame him. But where does fair come into matters of the heart?

Much, much later, when we young ones regaled each other with Mum's sins, we remembered her reaction (told to us by Mum herself) to the nurse who had hurried in with an X-ray showing that two babies, not one, were on the way. 'You'll be very pleased to know you're having twins, Mrs Sweetman,' was met with Mum's, 'I'm not pleased at all, thank you very much.'

'What a monster she is!' we chanted. 'How uncaring! What a bitch! No wonder we are all so fucked up!'

Not one of us thought: Jesus, the poor thing, she was still only in her thirties, her man was ill, her beautiful home was gone, she already had four children under five and was stuck back under her mother's roof. Of course she didn't want bloody twins! But by that time the female energy in the family had gotten so distorted that not one of us thought to support her, to try to understand.

DAD'S SIDE

Dad's family, the Sweetmans, were originally Norman and 'came over' in the twelfth century. Unlike the largely Protestant Anglo-Irish, the Normans were mainly Catholic and so often sided with the Catholic/Irish cause. Many were landowners, brewers, lawyers.

Grandfather trained as a barrister, but was so shy, according to Mum, that he never once practised. Luckily for him he inherited money and was able to set up as a 'gentleman farmer' in 'Derrybawn House', a beautiful Italianate early 1800s Georgian mansion in Glendalough, home of the earliest monastic settlements in Co. Wicklow. 'Derrybawn' had its own mountains, ancient oak woods, rivers, parkland, farm and gardens. Once ensconced, Grandfather set about developing a pedigree Friesian cattle herd – the first in Ireland – and raising a large family. Perhaps, more accurately, giving Granny a large family to raise.

Grandfather was a seriously right-wing Catholic, supporting some very strange über-Catholic organisations – the Knights of Columbanus and the Order of Malta. He also had a legendary temper. Mum remembers the first time the dining room in Derrybawn mysteriously cleared, with six-foot-plus men suddenly plunging out through the French doors as Grandfather began his tic-tic-tic noises, the prelude to one of his explosions. Weathering such storms meant that Mum didn't scare easily.

Staying in Derrybawn and heavily pregnant with her first child, she was cycling down to The Royal Hotel in Glendalough to meet Gaga for dinner one evening when Grandfather, who considered The Royal a den of low-life iniquity, came scorching down the avenue after her wielding his walking stick: 'NOBODY FROM THIS FAMILY IS ALLOWED GO TO THE ROYAL HOTEL!' Mum, unfazed, replied, 'I am going to meet my mother in The Royal Hotel for dinner, and there's nothing you can do about it Mr Sweetman' and cycled on.

Apart from Granny Sweetman, had anyone else ever stood up to him so? I think not.

Dad was midway in a big noisy family of five brothers – Paddy, Rory, Michael, Hugh and Dad – and six sisters – Peggy, Maureen, Catherine, Joan, Bon and Bid. All the boys were educated, entered the professions – solicitor, barrister, farmer, priest, etc. – got married and had children. Only one of 'the aunts' did – Aunt Catherine. Mum thought it outrageous. Not a single party thrown in their honour! Not a single attempt to get them 'out' and into the world, to find them careers, *husbands*! Very old-fashioned, was Mum's crisp verdict.

SEABANK

When Dad finally came home from the sanatorium in Switzerland, he and Mum were given a present of another house. This time it came from Mum's side of the family, or, more precisely, her father's sister, Winifred Stack. Winifred had had a busy past. First married to an RIC man, after he died she had married Austin Stack, the Irish revolutionary and republican on the anti-Treaty side, and later minister for justice under Éamon de Valera. She was a member of Cumann na mBan, the revolutionary women's branch of the Irish struggle, and had allowed her home, 'Seabank', to be used as a first-aid station, a locale for meetings, and a place to hide guns and men. Mum adored her.

It was at 'Seabank', looking out over Dublin Bay, that we became our own big, noisy, more or less functional family with me in the middle – four above and four below.

Oh 'Seabank', where happiness began. And ended.

It was there that Mum and Dad, on good terms again, gave dinner parties with roses cut from the garden in the centre of the dining table, a roast in the oven, a bottle of red wine opened and carefully decanted into the cut-glass Georgian decanter just washed in hot water and soap, their best dinner service and pungent Silvo'd candelabra on news-papers laid out on the kitchen table. Mum would be in a dress and wearing a necklace Dad had bought at Christmas.

It was also there that Mum got us ready for the hunt, me weak with nerves, the white shirt cold on goose-bumped skin and Mum saying, 'Remember to keep your seat.' Mum trialling a bay hunter the week before and Dad saying, 'Just look at your Mother's seat.' Mum cantering around a lumpy field looking like a stranger – young, confident, whole, at ease.

It was from 'Seabank' that the big ones went off to boarding school, us middle ones doing homework at the nursery table, the little ones upstairs in the drawing room with Mum and Dad. It was in the hangar-sized garage that we kept the Connemara ponies, riding them, fat-tummied, farting from too much oats and grass, out across miles of wrinkled sands, the sea a ribbon of aquamarine in the distance. It was here that Dad cooked Sunday breakfast on the big stove, pockets bulging with eggs: 'How many takers for eggs have I got today?'

Me, Dad, me, me, me!

It was at 'Seabank' that we had our own little empire: meat delivered in bloody brown-paper parcels tied with string by the butcher's boy on his black bike; coal delivered on a horse and cart, the coalmen's eyes blue diamonds in blackened faces, blackened sacks tied around their shoulders like shawls; and the dry-cleaning carried carefully up the front steps in crackling paper by a man in suede shoes, Mum saying they were 'co-respondent shoes'. Dad laughing, his head thrown back, me saying, 'What does co-respondent mean?' Mum and Dad exchanging glances, more laughter, the laundry delivered and collected in big, creaking wicker baskets in a red van loudly bannered 'SWASTIKA LAUNDRY'.

In the summer, Mum and Dad gave drinks parties up-stairs, with us children out all day in the garden, building dens and hideouts, and playing games that went on for days. My brother teaching us how to play cricket: LBW! Catch the bloody ball, would you? It hurts! The hurtling ball, brick-heavy inside its tight leather stitching. My brother teaching us how to box, how to use his air gun.

The last summer before disaster hit was a scorcher, every-one brown, in shorts, summer dresses, linen jackets, out in the garden under the big old greengage tree from June till September.

In the black-and-white photos, I look as if I'm turning into a boy. I wanted to be a boy. I would be a boy. I would ditch all girliness and save my family from the storm to come.

In the same photos Mum has a strained expression, her face a Modigliani, inscrutable, tilted, holding my younger sister; Dad, festooned with brown-skinned children, looking across anxiously at her.

BEFORE AND AFTER

Then, when I was ten, my little sister, Cathy, died.

Mum remembered a sort of 'attack' one night during her pregnancy but this was pre-scan days and only when Cathy was born was it discovered that she had 'reversed ventricles' and a hole in her heart. A 'blue baby'. Being so vulnerable, she crept in under Mum's defences and for the six short years of her life she was Mum and Dad's main focus, the love of their lives. In a desperate last-ditch gamble to try to mend Cathy's failing health, Mum had taken her over to a hospital in London for an operation. She died on the operating table. Dad hadn't had the strength – or the courage? – to go over and be there with them.

Mum came home alone. She got into bed. And didn't speak to any of us for what seemed to my ten-year-old self like 100 years. She particularly didn't speak to Dad.

A fault line, one that had opened inside Mum when her own father had been killed, now yawned. Mum froze to the bone, travelling alone into a profound depression. Dad, broken with grief and guilt, peered in helpless.

Before Cathy's death we were a family – Mum, Dad, one brother, eight sisters, beautiful old house by the sea with acres of garden, orchards, espaliered peaches on a warm granite wall, the front garden, the rose garden, the pussy willow orchard, the vegetable garden and the apple orchard. Life involved us sitting on the floor in the evenings, drying our hair in front of the banked turf fire in the drawing room, the long dark turves leaning in over the vermilion flames like upturned currachs, eating corn on the cob straight from Dad's vegetable garden, hot butter running down our fingers, Mum one side, Dad the other. Mum after supper in front of the fire, reading us the classics: *Little Women, Robinson Crusoe, Little Lord Fauntleroy, Tom Brown's School Days, The Red Badge of Courage*, all of Charles Dickens, Jane Austen, and Daniel Defoe. Dad listening, watching, enjoying. Huge, delicious roasts every Sunday with lashings of hot gravy, big trays of roast potatoes, mashed potatoes, vegetables, fruits, all from the garden. Ice cream! Children's parties, visits to Gaga, weekends in Derrybawn. Aunt Maureen chasing a bat around the bedroom with a tennis racket at two in the morning. Us leaning in over the stable door, eyeing the gigantic bull all muscle and steam and snort. Piano lessons with Aunt Bon. Granny at the piano after dinner, an Edwardian lady in silk chiffon floor-length dress, softest blue cardigan and pearls: 'Be-e-lieve me if all those endearing young charms', everyone singing including the adults. Hanging out in the dairy with Aunt Bid, helping her churn, every surface sluiced, spotless, the air rich with wet butter glistening with oil, thick cream, warm milk straight from the Friesians. Winter hunting, getting ready, white shirt pressed, jodhpurs brushed, hard hat brushed, inside butterflies. Summer gymkhanas, the rich smells of horse dung, tea from flasks, churned grass. Visiting cousins, arguments, shouting, charades and dinner dances for the older ones. Month-long summer breaks when Dad got holidays and he and Mum rented a house in the country, Connemara or Kerry, decamping *en famille* for a month's heaven with Dad around, Mum happier, everyone happier, days to explore, swim, new beaches, lakes or rivers every day, sea swims in freezing, salty, green-blue water, lake swims in silky brown, Dad fishing, picnics with cold sausages in tinfoil, hard-boiled eggs, a twist of salt in greaseproof paper, white-bread sandwiches, tomato or egg, make up your mind, quick, I'm starving, hot sweet tea from the flask, skin prickling with sunburn, climbing mountains – only one more ridge to go! – collecting blackberries, meeting strange boys with their hot country breath at evening ceilidhs, cousins visiting from England, blond-skinned, blond-haired and a little nervous.

After Cathy's death we were Mum, Dad, brother, seven sisters, all in whited-out shock, in a shit, horrible house in middle-class suburbia because Dad wouldn't stay at 'Seabank' – too many memories, he sobbed, while Mum silent-shrieked MEMORIES ARE ALL WE'VE GOT NOW! Dad gone, like a skeleton, a cut-out man barely able to breathe, heralding our new abode – 'Here we are!' I remember clenched red bricks, thorn bushes, thin gravel, earth that smelt of dog shit. Ponies gone, hunting gone, garden gone, vegetables gone, peaches espaliered against a warm granite wall gone, sea gone, sand gone, cantering farting ponies over ridged wet sand gone, salty wind cutting your face gone, Sunday roasts gone, big delicious Sunday breakfasts with everything piled up high on the oval dinner plate gone, big brother and big sister gone, sunny summer days under the greengage tree with garden chairs pulled out of the greenhouse and freshly whitely painted gone. Mum gone. Mum in bed day after day, sister number two standing at the end of the bed yelling, 'YOU HAVE TO GET UP!' 'No,' says Mum, shifting further down the bed, our no-to-everything Mum: No, no, no, no, no, no, no. Sister number two yelling at us. Air gone, hope gone, little sister Cathy gone gone gone.

Before it had been Mum and Dad suns at the centre, children planets held in their respective orbits around them. Now it was Mum lost in the frozen dark, Dad frantically sending out distress signals. The more we starving young ones orbited around Dad for warmth, the more frozen, isolated and bitter Mum became. We were a household crowded with females, but the chief female had withdrawn and so the balance in the family between male and female energy became fatally distorted. There was no therapy for Mum. No counselling. No help. Just the GP, a family friend, who was told to 'buzz off' when he stood uncertainly in the doorway of Mum's room.

BOARDING SCHOOL

Three months before Cathy died, my sister and I had been sent off to boarding school.

The first time I dipped my toe into therapy, years later, I went straight back to walking down a long corridor, a nun beside me, my stiff new shoes echoing on the polished cement, marble-effect floor, my head blank but, weirdly, buzzing at the same time.

'Walking into shock,' the therapist said, delighted with all the imagery. 'Classic.'

'You mean I went into shock going to boarding school?'

'Naturally!'

Two things I remember before Mum and Dad drove us down: a fortnight of mounting nausea, a strange, removed-from-reality feeling. Thinking: they cannot be sending us away from home – away from the family, away from supper, away from the ponies, away from the evenings in the drawing room, away from our dog Scutch, away from 'Seabank', away from the wrinkled sands – *can* they?

The other memory is standing in front of the mirror on Mum's desk, my eldest sister giving me and my sister pudding-bowl haircuts. We went from pretty pre-teen girls with 'Irish blonde' hair to sexless (confused) choirboys with mud-coloured bobs. Was she trying to make us ugly? Several days later, off we went with our terrible haircuts and our trunks, school lists taped to the inside lids: two pairs of navy outdoor knickers, four pairs of white indoor knickers, two pairs of brown knee socks, two detachable white collars, one navy Sunday dress, two day uniforms, two jumpers, three vests, one sports skirt, one toothbrush, one flannel, one hand towel, one bath towel and two flannel nightdresses.

The morning Cathy died, a nun pulled us out of the refectory queue and said, 'Your sister Cathy died this morning.' Then she told us to rejoin the queue for maths. We were not brought home for Cathy's funeral.

When we came home for the holidays everything that had been our family was over – Mum, Dad, the older ones, all cowed inside a tragedy we hadn't been there for. Estranged at boarding school, we were now strangers at home.

With a young person's blunt selfishness, I thought that I understood a little of Mum and Dad's loss with Cathy's death, but mostly felt alone and bewildered inside my own loss of them (to grief) and loss of home (to grief and to boarding school).

Oh good God, boarding school – how did anyone ever think it was an acceptable, desirable, character-building thing to do to young human beings? When we get more civilised I'm certain we'll see it as akin to foot-binding in traditional China. Take a young, unsuspecting creature and, while they are smiling trustingly, bend their little foot back on itself with one savage twist, smashing tiny bones, cracking the arch. Next, bind up the mutilation and make them walk crippled for the rest of their life. Then, cruellest twist of all, make them believe it all was, and is, for the best.

Arguably boarding school is worse, as it involves mutilation of the self.

No wonder my ten-year-old self went into shock.

I hated the smells that didn't smell like home. I hated the harsh surfaces, everything reeking of floor polish. I hated the thunder and clatter of the refectory. I hated the food boiled up in the industrial-sized kitchen smelling of cabbage and floor cloths. I hated the narrow beds lined up in the dormitories; the huge, badly shuttered windows; the nun in the morning annunciating the prayer, then hurrying down the centre aisle, whipping back the white curtains, whipping back your bed covers, 'Up! Up!', clanging her bell. I hated the way the older nuns' false teeth whistled when they spoke. I hated their colourless spectacle frames. I hated the gargantuan size of everything, the huge grey prison of a building, the endless corridors, the massive stairs, the ceilings that seemed to be hundreds of feet high, the great lonely playing fields and the cawing rooks descending in clouds at dusk against grey skies. I hated that there were no men, no uncles, no cousins, no brothers, no boys. Nobody to turn to when things got too intense. Nobody to say, 'Cut it out', when things got too bitchy. Nobody to say, 'Oh relax.'

Underpinning the unhappiness was the brutal unanswerable question: how could this new reality actually be? How could it be that from now on, i.e. forever, thirty-five weeks out of every fifty-two would be spent away from home, here in this prison run by all-female strangers, with all the adults agreeing it was a terrific thing, a fantastic opportunity, a gift?

The scariest thing is, you adapt. You develop what psychiatrists now call a 'Strategic Survival Personality' or a 'false self', a 'Miss Jolly Hockey Sticks' persona – a self who goes out into the world and does stuff loudly and jollily, while the real you, the shocked and frozen you, disappears ever deeper inside.

The more one adapted, the more the adults proclaimed: 'How marvellous! She's come round at last! They all do, you know! Well done, Reverend Mother! Bravo, Mistress of Studies!'

I turned into 'Miss Jolly Hockey Sticks'. Then I was lost.

Years after leaving school I was coming up the front steps to a children's party at Mum's, baby in arms, toddler at my side. A friend from the old alma mater, also invited by Mum, appeared. In between chivvying toddler, shifting babe from one arm to another, ditto baby kit, going chat, chat, chat, chat, how are you, how are things, etc., in a flush of bonhomie I said, 'It wasn't that bad, was it?' I can't remember my old school friend's reply because Mum looked up from her chair by the fire: 'Don't you remember how you used to cry?'

Talk about coming back down to earth with a fucking crash.

THE MADRASAH

Boarding school went like this: up at seven to a loudly called prayer from the dormitory nun. Tearing back of curtains, etc., nun calling 'Up! Up!' Slippers on, stand in line in the middle of the dorm to wash face with cold wet flannel and cold wet water at one basin, teeth done separately, spitting into blue tooth mug. Back to cubicle, get dressed, put veil on and file down to chapel. Hour-long mass, then a stampede to the refectory for breakfast. Their worst-ever breakfast concoction? Stewed cooking apples with cornflakes gone blotting-paper soggy on top. Otherwise, lumpy porridge, bread and jam. On Sunday, eggs fried to rubber, hanks of bacon with the hair still on, tea. After breakfast, lessons till 11 a.m. break. Fifteen minutes in the yard, then back to class till lunchtime. Most hideous lunch? Sausages cooked to the texture of a dead elephant scrotum with warm mashed potatoes, the eyes still in, made without salt or butter.

Letters – oh, precious letters! – were handed out after lunch so that the Mistress of Studies had time to read and, if necessary, censor them. The best one was on my sixteenth birthday from my very dashing boyfriend at boarding school in England with a 45 rpm copy of 'Happy Birthday Sweet Sixteen' – 'since you've grown up your future is sewn up' – the little disc played to near death in the recreation hall every evening, my whole class going demented with the romance of it.

After lunch there was forty-five minutes' recreation: hockey or tennis outside, if it wasn't raining; inside if it was. Lessons for the afternoon. Tea. Study for two hours. Then supper – more boiled sausages, the smell of them pervading the whole school. Half-hour recreation after supper. Dormitory. Bed.

Saturday was confession day. Sunday was benediction in the afternoon with incense, flowers and hymns, as well as an extra-long morning mass with white veils.

When I tried to explain it all, years later, to my darling daughter, she listened carefully. 'So basically it was a Madrasah?' (A college strictly for religious instruction.)

Oh my God, I thought, she's right!

Within an hour of arriving at the school your 'home' clothes were taken away. From then until the morning of the holidays – Halloween, Christmas, Easter and summer – you had no access to them. Books had to be passed by the Mistress of Studies, otherwise you could go to the library – a strange, frigid room with books of saints' lives and a handful of classics held behind locked glass. To make a phone call you had to get permission from the Mistress of Studies – was someone at home ill? – then beg, borrow and steal the coins you would need for the big, coin-eating phone outside the downstairs 'parlour'.

The parlour that smelt of floor wax and polish and was

where your parents, or very occasionally an uncle and aunt, and once the parents of a boyfriend, another time Granny and my godmother, waited while you were called: Visitors! Visits were a welcome break from routine but were strange in their own way. Even your parents seemed altered by being in the nuns' world, by the all-pervading polish, by the atmosphere of shuttered-up, all-female religiosity.

On Sunday mornings a special place was set in the parlour for the priest and the female religiosity went into overdrive. 'The priest's breakfast', a thing of legend, was carried in on a dining plate by the 'sisters', or the more lowly nuns who came into the convent without a dowry and did the dirty work – the cooking, cleaning, gardening and washing. Oh, how the sisters fussed around the priest, proud of their massive plate mounded with fried eggs, sausages, bacon, black and white pudding, mushrooms, tomatoes and fried bread; so proud of their priest, their man.

THE NIGHT BEFORE
I WAS EXPELLED

The night before I was expelled, the school was called to assemble in the study hall. In front of the entire school – juniors, day girls, seniors, prefects – I was called up to the podium by the Mistress of Studies. There was such a pounding in my ears that I don't remember anything of the long speech she made, just the words, 'and will be expelled from this school'. She might as well have said, 'and will be hanged by the neck until she is dead'.

You could have heard a hair kirby drop.

I was led out. On the landing outside, another nun said I was to go to my cubicle and stay there without talking to ANYONE, not even to my sister. Was that quite clear? In the morning I would be accompanied downtown to the Dublin train by one of the lay teachers. Was that quite clear?

Actually nothing was clear. A hideous and malignant machinery seemed to have started up and was going to tear me apart, spit me out, no matter what I did or said.

Wasn't I ashamed, the nun wanted to know? Wasn't I horrified at the upset I was causing my parents, to whom she had just spoken and who were absolutely devastated at the news? WHAT WERE MY PARENTS GOING TO SAY? Wasn't I disgusted with myself for bringing this on my family, particularly since my dear mother and father had already been through so much sorrow and tragedy with the death of my sister? Wasn't I dismayed that I was doing this to them after all the sacrifices they had made to send me to this school in the first place? AND THIS IS HOW I REPAID THEM?

On the train the next day I stood in the space between the carriages, the window open, the rails below visible in the crack between the carriages, trying to summon the courage to open the hefty door and fling myself out into the rushing outside, into death.

I was just seventeen. All I could think of was killing myself. For a ridiculously small misdemeanour that I hadn't even done! Madrasah indeed.

At home, Mum was waiting.

'Did you do it?'

It was the first time anyone had asked the question. '*No.*'

And that was it. Mum went to see the nuns. I got some extra days' holidays and back I went with everyone else for our final term and exams.

Nothing more was ever said. By the nuns. By the other girls. Or by me. That was how things worked. You did not dare to risk setting that terrible machinery in motion again. You did not dare fight for your good name, to appeal the injustice of it all. Oh no, no, no.

What had happened was innocent enough: it had been our second-last term at school and a lot of high jinks had been going on. In one dormitory some girls had discovered a small hole where a knot had fallen out of the wooden partition separating the girls from a nun's cubicle; in this case a novice, or young nun, who slept in the dorm with us. There was much merriment, pushing and shoving to get a peek into this forbidden territory. I remember a cubicle no bigger than ours with a bed, a bedside locker, a washbowl and jug, and a chair. A cell. The following afternoon, during tea break, intense excitement: the nun was in her cubicle and doing her ablutions! A whispered commentary was relayed to the five or six girls clamouring to get a look-see. Someone giggled. There was a rush and a crash as the nun realised something was happening, then understood what was happening and fled into the corridor. Before you could say *Te rogamus, audi nos*, one of the big nuns barrelled into the dorm, red in the face, rosary flying. Commotion as girls fled, then I was grabbed – 'Rosita Sweetman!' – and hauled off.

The nuns were after a victim and I would do nicely. To be fair, I was usually at the centre of whatever mild bits of craziness we got up to. The girl who was actually at the peephole stayed shtum, as did all the others.

Ho hum.

BOYS BOYS BOYS BOYS BOYS

Boys. Boys, boys, boys, boys, boys. The more we pushed on into puberty, the more we thought about boys.

At home, before boarding school had taken over, boys hadn't been a problem. There was Dad, my brother, cousins, lots of uncles and a friend/boy my own age (ten) up the road. At Irish College, which I'd gone to before boarding school, boys and girls were treated with the same rough-and-ready routine – classes in Gaelic, swims in the Irish sea, long walks in the winter with a peeled turnip as a snack (I swear), and ceilidh dances on Saturday evenings.

It wasn't until boarding school proper that boys became the 'other'. An 'occasion of sin'.

Once a year the seniors attended a musical in the town, along with the seniors from the local boys boarding school. 'Oh what a beautiful morning, oh what a beautiful day, I've got a wonderful feeling, everything's going my way.' While the powdered and wigged ones up on stage belted out American musicals, praising prairies and sunshine, celebrating a reckless bonhomie we'd never even dreamed of, the rain dashed down outside and we craned our heads in the darkness to catch glimpses of the boys, led in after we had already been seated. When the curtain came down we were hurried out again and whisked off in buses before the boys milled out onto the road, desperate to catch a glimpse of us.

At home things weren't much better.

Dinner dances were the 'thing' among the middle classes, where sons and daughters could mingle and meet under the watchful eyes of parents. You were pressed into a hideous dress, usually a hand-me-down, kitten-heel shoes and a hair-do your sister assured you was 'very Hayley Mills', then led off to the slaughter feeling as unlike yourself as you could imagine.

Double doors between drawing room and dining room in the host house were opened, furniture pushed back, floor-boards French chalked, an older brother or sister brought in to supervise the record player, and you waited for a pimply damp youth in an evening suit to come and ask you to dance.

Intimacy was encouraged in the last few dances where you and the now profusely sweating youth would have to tread the boards with a coin held between your foreheads. The first couple to drop the coin left the dance, and so on, until only one couple survived and thereby won.

The adults thought it all terrifically funny as they laid into the punch.

You hoped for, and dreaded, a snog on the porch. You hoped for it so you would have something to tell your friends; you dreaded it because the boys were usually as clueless as you were as to what to do.

We left boarding school criminally clueless. Even when

we were in sixth year, lusty seventeen- and eighteen-year-olds, *The Irish Times* was considered too racy for our delicate minds.

Sexual advice at home was scant. Mum was too depressed. The only sex education I remember is her coming into our bedroom a couple of weeks before we went to boarding school, very cross, closing the door too sharply behind her. In one hand she held up a white strap that looked like something we might put on the ponies, in the other an oblong bandage, looped at either end. 'You'll start getting the curse soon. When you do you'll have to wear one of these.'

The 'curse'?

Wear one of these?

Bleeding?

Every month?

Mum didn't wait for a question-and-answer session; none of the older ones had even mentioned it.

Sweet Jesus.

THE DARK AGES

So yes, we, and almost all of Ireland, were still in the dark ages. Complete ignorance on all matters sexual was rigidly enforced. Pregnancy 'outside marriage' was regarded as the end of the world. For many girls, it literally was the end of their lives. Working-class and country girls were packed off to Mother and Baby Homes. The luckier middle-class girls were sent off to London to have their pregnancy in shame and secrecy, give up the baby for adoption and return home as if nothing had happened; but at least they weren't incarcerated in Magdalene Laundries for the rest of their lives. The weirdest part was that the parents of the 'ruined' girls stood by and let it happen. Made damn bloody sure it happened. Anything was better than Mammy and Daddy's good name getting a bit of shite on it.

Sex was the taboo. It was allowed, thank you very much, for a heterosexual couple who were married and wanted to make babies. Any other kind of sex, even for married heterosexual couples, was taboo. Even married couples weren't expected to take pleasure in it. Pleasure! The very idea!

OF COURSE married couples should not be FUCKING EACH OTHER JOYOUSLY just for the sake of it! What a FILTHY AND TWISTED IDEA! Sex was designed by ALMIGHTY GOD for the PROPAGATION

OF THE SPECIES – and nothing else, OKAY?

OKAY?

Not that the nuns would have dreamed of saying 'Okay.' Or 'fucking joyously' for that matter.

Ireland was 98 per cent patriarchal, inward-looking, stagnated, puritanical, Catholic. There was a tiny (mainly) Protestant Anglo-Irish elite who went their own way, but everyone else went to confession. Everyone went to mass. Everyone played nice Catholic GAA games. Everyone went to Catholic schools and Catholic universities run by the Catholic hierarchy. Everyone was baptised in the Catholic Church, made their first communion ('a bride of Christ') in the Church, and later their confirmation. Marriages took place in the Church *and only in the Church*. Funerals took place in the Church. *And only in the Church.*

Looking back at a recently published photographic study of the 1950s, it's striking how men crowd the photos – in the workplace, at the football games, in the bars, at the races, on the roads, in the army, in the judges' box at the horse show.[1] Where were the women? Where *were* they? Mostly they were at home, drowning in babies.

During the summer before sixth year, one of my sister's boyfriends took me to the cinema and stuck his (very large) tongue down my throat. One part of me knew this must be

---

1   Lensmen Photographic Archive, *The 1950s: Ireland in Pictures* (O'Brien Press, Dublin, 2013).

a 'French kiss' and was pleased to notch up another piece of 'sexperience'. Afterwards, being clamped to his back as he thundered through the leafy burbs on his motorbike, my face turning to liquid rubber from the G-force, was proper fun; the horrible French kiss seemed his price for the gallivants, extracted without preliminaries or romance.

Everyone was repressed. Everyone was puritanical – if I can't have fun and an easy conscience about myself and my bodily desires, then sure as hell's fire neither can you.

Underneath, of course, most people were scared, longing for joy, good times and love.

When The Rolling Stones came to Dublin in 1965 for their first gigs, we all nearly lost our minds. Jesus! Here were guys openly revelling in their sexuality, in their bodies, driving us to states of complete frenzy with their come-to-bed eyes, lewd lyrics, pounding music, gyrating snake hips, their sheer goddamn delight in being alive, sexy, male, *rude*. We wept, stormed the stage, tried to tear their clothes off, fainted.

By 1966 the years of repression, fear, ignorance, hypocrisy and puritanism led to Ireland having the lowest marriage rate in Europe, with the highest number of children per marriage: nine, ten, twelve children per Catholic couple was not uncommon. Women enjoying sex, even within marriage, was not spoken about, not even considered. A married woman could be 'cold and frigid or warm and pregnant', wrote academic Tom Inglis in his paper titled 'Origins and

Legacies of Irish Prudery'.[2]

Post-colonial cripples that we were, we loved authority. As a feminist and republican socialist activist of the day, Rosamond Jacob, wrote:

> In spite of – or perhaps because of – our perpetual fight for national freedom, the principle of authority has ten times more weight with us than the principle of liberty. We love authority. We don't feel comfortable except when we are told by our own native authorities what we may do and what we may not, what cinema pictures we may see, what Sunday papers we may read, what dances we may dance, what men we may speak to.[3]

Post-independence censorship of books and films was rigid. The first censorship board here was actually called 'The Committee on Evil Literature'. Very Gothic. Questioning the rate at which the censors – two priests, of course – were banning books, Senator Sir John Keane said 1,600 books had been banned in twenty years and suggested that the priests would have to be reading three books a week each, as well as carrying out all of their normal duties. Was this even possible?

---

2   Inglis, Tom, 'Origins and Legacies of Irish Prudery: Sexuality and Social Control in Modern Ireland', https://researchrepository.ucd.ie/handle/10197/5112.
3   Steiner-Scott, Liz, 'Female Activists: Irish Women and Change 1900–1960', *History Ireland*, Issue 2, Vol. 11 (Summer 2003), https://www.historyireland.com/20th-century-contemporary-history/female-activists-irish-women-and-change-1900-1960.

Brendan Behan's *Borstal Boy* was banned. As were Salinger's *The Catcher in the Rye*; *Brave New World* by Aldous Huxley; *The Ginger Man* by J. P. Donleavy; *The Second Sex* by Simone de Beauvoir; and Edna O'Brien's debut novel, *The Country Girls*. As Donal Fallon notes, in his *Hidden History* series, Archbishop McQuaid was so outraged by *The Country Girls* that he rushed to then Minister for Justice Charles Haughey and demanded its immediate banning. Both of them agreed, said Edna, 'that the book was filth and should not be allowed inside any decent home'.[4] This was a smear on Irish womanhood! This must be banned! Now! *The Country Girls* was duly banned, even burned in O'Brien's hometown.

Of course censorship was not, is not, an Irish-only phenomenon; the Irish twist was censorship's obsession, thanks to the Church, with sex.

One of censorship's chief aims was to ensure that not a sniff of an alternative life reached Ireland's shores – and this was largely successful. TD Oliver J. Flanagan's famous remark that 'there was no sex in Ireland before television' holds a kernel of truth. No public discussion or display of a lifestyle different to the one imposed by the Church was tolerated. The Church controlled the discourse around sexuality, and priests put forward sex education tips such as FEAR, formulated in 1960: if kisses are Frequent, Enduring

---

4   *The Irish Times*, 5 November 2018.

and Ardent, there can hardly be any Reason for them.

Writer Anne Enright, now professor of fiction at University College Dublin, in an interview on RTÉ Radio with Miriam O'Callaghan, described chatting with her daughter recently about the Ireland she, and her parents, had grown up in. Her daughter queried how on earth people were made to obey all the nonsensical rules set out by the Church. Enright's reply was to the point: 'people obeyed because *they thought they would go to Hell*'.[5]

They did! *We* did! Until we got to travelling and saw how others lived.

Crucially, whether the priests and the politicians liked it or not, all along the east coast of Ireland people had had access to British TV since the 1950s. Censorship couldn't stop 'leakage' from BBC and ITV transmitters across the Irish Sea. In his 2014 paper *Television in Ireland: History from a Mediated Centre*, Edward Brennan wrote that 'in 1955 there were an estimated 4,000 television sets in Ireland with fifty new sets being sold every week'.[6]

By 1961 we had our own TV station: RTÉ. The old hegemony of an infallible Church and State, particularly on matters sexual, was crumbling.

---

5   *Sunday with Miriam*, 11 November 2018, https://www.rte.ie/radio1/
     sunday-with-miriam/programmes/2018/1111/1010148-sunday-
     with-miriam-sunday-11-november-2018/?clipid=102975563.
6   Brennan, Edward, 'Television in Ireland: A History from the Medi-
     ated Centre' (ICA Conference, Japan, June 2016), p. 7.

Colm Tóibín remembers watching 'the telly' with his family:

> Down in Enniscorthy when I was a lad we all sat glued to it. We were often glued by embarrassment that someone was talking about sex: there were older people in the room who didn't like sex being talked about. If *The Late Late Show* had not existed it is highly possible that many people would have lived their lives in Ireland in the twentieth century without ever having heard anyone talking about sex. If any other programme had mentioned sex, it would have been turned off. Turn that rubbish off. But nobody ever turned *The Late Late Show* off.[7]

Still, in my own life I was just about to be liberated – from boarding school, from the nuns. As the school chant went: 'No more Irish, no more French, no more sitting on a hard old bench. Kick up tables, kick up chairs, kick Mother Rita down the stairs.'

That final day I ran so hard up the railway platform that I dropped my case, tripped over it and landed – much to his amusement, goddammit – spreadeagled at Dad's feet.

It was 1965. Life was about to begin.

Hurray!

---

7   Tóibín, Colm, 'Gay Byrne: Irish Life as Cabaret', *The Crane Bag*, Vol. 8, No. 2 (1984), pp. 65–9.

A HISTORY OF 'UPPITY WOMEN' IN IRELAND

SECTION II

WOMEN AND THE
CATHOLIC CHURCH

Of course men have been horribly damaged by the Catholic Church, but it's the Church's deeply misogynistic attitude to women that must interest me most.

For centuries, 'woman' has represented a peerless scapegoat for the Church. Woman is Eve/Evil, woman is temptation, woman is darkness personified. Through woman everything that is 'sinful' came into the world.

Women, said the Church Fathers, are the root of all evil.

It started with Christianity's foundation story, the Garden of Eden, informing us that a) woman was created from a man's rib, and b) she, aka Eve, far from being grateful, then tempted man, Adam, to sin by persuading him to eat the fruit of the tree of knowledge being proffered by the Devil, handily disguised as a snake (a snake, get it?), and thereby c) she plunged all of us, forever, into Original Sin. Since the beginning, the Church has never let up on its anti-woman propaganda.

Woman, they assured us, was less than man, having been made from his rib; clearly she was also a good deal less, morally speaking, having suckered him into eating the Devil's apple. Or as Tertullian, one of the early 'Fathers' of the Catholic Church (AD 155–220) put it, 'God's sentence hangs still over all your sex ... You are the devil's gateway.' Or later, warming to his theme, 'Woman is a temple built over a sewer.'[1]

Lovely.

Or take a fourth-century archbishop of Constantinople: 'God maintained the order of each sex by dividing the business of human life into two parts and assigned the more necessary and beneficial aspects to the man and the less important, inferior matters to the woman.'[2]

Another early father of the Church, St Augustine (354–430 AD), a lusty rake in his youth ('Give me chastity and continence but not yet'), became thunderously anti-female and wondered: 'Why was woman created at all?' Also: 'Man is fertile and perfectly formed, and contributes soul to the offspring, whereas woman is infertile and deformed, and contributes body to the offspring.'[3]

Then there's St Albertus Magnus of the thirteenth century: 'One must be on one's guard with every woman, as if she were a poisonous snake and the horned devil ... in evil and perverse doings woman is cleverer, that is, slyer, than man.'[4]

---

1   Robertson, Pat, 'Twenty Vile Quotes Against Women', https://valerietarico.com/2013/07/01/mysogynistquoteschurchfathers/.

2   Mowczko, Marg, 'Misogynistic Quotations from Church Fathers and Reformers', https://margmowczko.com/misogynist-quotes-from-church-fathers/.

3   Just, Ashley N., 'The Catholic Church: Shaping the Roles of Medieval Women', https://pdxscholar.library.pdx.edu/younghistorians/2014/oralpres/16/.

4   Robertson, Pat, 'Twenty Vile Quotes Against Women', https://valerietarico.com/2013/07/01/mysogynistquoteschurchfathers/.

Not all priests, nuns or bishops in the Catholic Church have been misogynistic bastards terrified of women, but, looking back, the Church's misogyny has been an extraordinarily powerful component of the patriarchy's programme to assert control over women. It is a power and prejudice that women have suffered under and fought against up to this day.

'THE BURNING TIMES'

Many feminists would now argue that it was centuries of vicious anti-woman propaganda propagated by the Church that paved the way for 'the burning times' of the Middle Ages. This was a period of history when hundreds of thousands of women – many of them midwives, herbalists and healers – were burned as 'witches'. This was a time when State and Church interests demanded a 'pro-natalism' or pro-birth agenda, after years of war, internecine strife and plagues in Europe had decimated their populations. 'Witches', usually the 'wise women' of the villages, were guilty, according to pope and State, of hindering 'men from performing the sexual act and women from conceiving' (contraception), or had 'slain infants yet in the mother's womb' (abortion), indicating that women herbalists who helped other women control the size of their families were to be the target.[1]

Lurid tales of witches abounded: of them fucking the Devil, kissing the Devil's anus, eating babies, and making the crops fail. A witch-hunt began with the suspect being accused, taken from her home, stripped naked, shaved of all of her hair, including her pubic hair, before being led,

---

1   Papal Bull, see: https://en.wikipedia.org/wiki/Summis_desiderantes_
     affectibus.

walking backwards, hairless and naked, into the presence of the Inquisitor. The Inquisitor, male, richly clothed, highly educated – certainly ten thousand times more educated than she – a 'gentleman' the like of which she'd most likely never seen before, sat high above her on a raised dais and fired questions at her in Latin that she couldn't understand while she stood naked, shaved and terrified in front of him.

Days of torture followed. Women were bound using shackles that forced their bodies into positions that allowed easy access to their sexual organs. They were raped before being burnt alive. Specially designed tools were used to remove their breasts, burn their vulvae and rip their vaginas apart. 'Bridles' of iron forced spikes into their tongue and cheeks. Other lovelies included being buried alive in the Iron Maiden, dislocation on the rack, near drownings – otherwise known as 'duckings', which were basically early versions of waterboarding – whippings, application of finger and toe screws, floggings, and being hung up by their arms twisted behind their back for hours on end. A nice touch included the 'witch's' house and all her goods being confiscated to pay for her 'trial'.

The Dominican priests of the Inquisition and their henchmen were assiduously thorough. After three days of this, everyone 'confessed'.

It took 200 years, the burning of an estimated 60,000–80,000 women (though some believe the figure is much higher), and unaccountable anguish, grief and terror, before the Catholic Church could fully impose its writ: folk culture and folk medicine were officially banished and everything that wasn't Catholic doctrine was deemed heresy, devil worship, Satanism.

Of course many men died during 'the burning times'. Jews, Muslims, Protestants, Calvinists *et al.*, even an annoying braggart, not to mention the 'savages' in the colonies – all were targets for the 'holy' fathers – but the witch burnings that specifically targeted women and were 'a systematic killing of members of a specific gender' were surely gendercide.

Conveniently, with the practitioners of the old ways burnt to death, the Church gained control over women's sexuality, over conception, birth and abortion, with a nascent, now male-dominated, medical system at their service. Women's status within their communities as healers and midwives was stripped away. Women's power to control their fertility with the help of the herbalists and 'Eve's Herbs' was removed. It was going to take centuries, and an enormous amount of suffering, to get back some control.

THE LAST WITCH
BURNED IN IRELAND

As an exemplar of how conveniently the hysteria of witch trials killed and crushed women, the story of Bridget Cleary, 'the last witch burned in Ireland', has it all.

A beautiful, spirited, intelligent and independent young woman in 1890s deepest rural Ireland, Bridget Cleary was murdered by her husband, with her family either abetting or standing by terrified. The husband subsequently pleaded a 'faerie defence', thus avoiding the hangman's noose.

The case was a worldwide sensation. The press, particularly the British and unionist press, desperate to prove we Irish were manifestly not capable of governing ourselves and should not now, not ever, be granted Home Rule – then so close to being granted you could almost smell it – had a terrific time. We Irish were Hottentots! Cave dwellers! Such credulous ignorant savages that we still believed in faeries, and were prepared, for God's sake, to murder one of our own in the name of the faeries!

From the beginning Bridget Cleary seems to have stood out. Financially independent as a milliner and dressmaker, with her own sewing machine and a flock of hens whose eggs she sold, she was described as stylish, wearing hats with feathers in them, gold earrings and tailored clothes. As

Bridget's biographer, Angela Bourke, said, 'she wanted her share of the modern world'.[1]

At eighteen, she married Michael Cleary, almost ten years her senior and a cooper from the nearby town. One day she caught a chill walking three miles home from delivering eggs to a relative.

From the start her husband's response to her illness seems to have been highly charged. He went to the doctor. The doctor, a drunkard, didn't come. Then he went to a 'faerie doctor' and then to the priest. When the doctor came he said he found the patient suffering from bronchitis and in an excitable state. No wonder. The relative to whom she had been bringing eggs had arrived into the cottage and, perhaps out of guilt at causing her to become ill, pronounced: 'That is not Bridgey Boland', i.e. that is a 'changeling', someone brought in by the faeries.

It wasn't the first time her husband Cleary had tried this on. At the trial an aunt told the court how Bridget said her husband had 'thought to burn me about three months ago'; that he was 'trying to make a faerie out of me', going on, so poignantly, 'if I had my mother I would not be this way'.[2]

That evening, the tiny cottage crammed with relatives, Cleary locked the doors and attempted to force the faerie 'medicine' down his wife's throat. Young male cousins were

---

1   Bourke, Angela, *The Burning of Bridget Cleary: A True Story* (Penguin, London, 2001).
2   *Ibid.*, p. 66.

told to lie across her, hold her arms, hold her head down by the ears. Were these male cousins getting their rocks off, manhandling this proud young woman who thought she was 'above' them? Did they enjoy seeing her 'publicly humiliated' as Fin Dwyer of the *Irish History* podcast believes in his audio documentary? Screams were heard, with Michael Cleary yelling as he tried to push the medicine into her mouth, 'Take it you old bitch!'

'Away she go! Away she go!' shouted onlookers, encouraging the 'faerie' demons to leave. As Bridget resisted, the 'doctor' suggested 'laying down a good fire' and burning Bridget – that would surely make her behave. 'This is not my wife!' Cleary was shouting. 'This woman is too fine to be my wife.'[3]

By the time Bridget was brought back to her bed she was in a terrible state. Attacked by her husband, family and relatives, burnt, manhandled, her eyes streaming, her face and her nightclothes soaked with the contents of a chamber pot her husband had directed be thrown over her, her mouth torn, not to mention being sick and weak with bronchitis, she must have felt she'd landed in hell.

A day later Michael Cleary's father died, no doubt adding to his near-hysterical state.

Bridget had now been sick for eleven days, but got up

---

3   *Irish History Podcast*, 11 July 2016, https://irishhistorypodcast.ic/pod-cast-bridget-cleary-the-last-woman-burned-alive-in-ireland/.

and put on clean clothes. Two cousins helped her to dress: two petticoats, a navy shirt, a navy jacket, a white shawl and black stockings for her feet.

There was chat by the fire, cups of tea, and then the husband started up again. The faeries this, the faeries that. Incredibly, this young woman, who'd been almost killed two nights before, spoke back to her husband, saying, 'Your mother used to go with them (the faeries), that's why you think I'm going with them.'

'And did she?' asked the husband. Presumably you could have heard a hairpin drop.

'She did,' said the wife, 'two days.'[4]

Was it reckless bravado, or was it her way of fingering the man she probably knew by now was going, one way or another, to kill her?

Cleary went insane. Here was this woman, independent, beautiful, sassy and, worst of all, unafraid, saying in front of relatives and neighbours that his ma had gone with the faeries.

He instructed his wife to eat three pieces of bread and jam. 'In the name of God.' She managed two, but baulked at the third. He exploded. 'If you won't take it, down you will go.' He jumped at her. Knocked her to the floor. At the trial her aunt said there was a terrible crack and a scream as Bridget's head hit the floor. Then Cleary, kneeling on top

---

4   *The Irish Times*, 24 November 2016.

of her brandishing a burning stick from the fire, tried to shove the bread and jam down her throat. Bridget's cousin, Johanna, who gave evidence at the trial, said Cleary was screaming, 'Swallow it. Is it down? Is it down?' and that you could see bread come up again, 'with bloody froth' between Cleary's fingers.

The husband began tearing off his wife's clothes, leaving only her chemise. He grabbed a paraffin lamp, flinging the paraffin over her shouting, 'She's not my wife. She's an old deceiver sent in place of my wife.'

As the terrified relatives later testified, 'Bridget blazed up all in a minute.'[5]

The following days Cleary seems to have had a public meltdown, but was canny enough to get together a posse of the witnesses to the murder and force them up to a local 'faerie fort' from where he said his wife would emerge. Then one of the witnesses went to confession and the priest went to the police.

Bridget's body, naked except for a black stocking and one gold earring, was found. It was so badly burnt that the flesh had gone from the legs and lower torso, the skeleton exposed, her head in a sack, 'the features showing the terrible suffering she had been through'.[6]

At his trial Cleary made his 'faerie defence' and the

5   Bourke (2001), p. 109.
6   *Ibid.*

press went mad. Ireland was pilloried the world over. Cleary escaped the noose and was found guilty of manslaughter only. Poor burned Bridget was hurried into an unmarked grave in the dead of night by the Royal Irish Constabulary. Cleary went to jail for fifteen years.

Of course faerie lore and customs were still widely believed in in rural Ireland, but Bridget's horrific death was surely about the removal of an 'inconvenient' woman at the hands of an abusive man, while the patriarchy once again turned a blind eye. As a neighbour, now an old lady, Peggy O'Brien, said in Adrian McCarthy's 2005 documentary *Fairy Wife*, 'I think myself the man was only looking for an excuse to get rid of her and he played on the minds of the innocent people.'

And so the story goes on. Violence against women is endemic and domestic. In the UK in 2017 one woman was killed every 2.6 days. Femicide Watch and Women's Aid, both here and in the UK, say that 88 per cent of women who are murdered are killed by an 'intimate partner' – a husband, lover, boyfriend or ex-boyfriend. And not a faerie to be seen anywhere.

THE GREAT HUNGER

Still, how was it that we in Ireland were held prisoner for so long by a rigid, puritanical and anti-woman Catholicism?

How?

For the answers I believe we're going to have to go back to the famine, *An Gorta Mór* (the Great Hunger), of the nineteenth century. It was an event as seismic as 1916 and the fight for independence, if not more so.

Ireland was the first country colonised by the British. It was in Ireland that successive British rulers tested and honed the brutalities common to subsequent colonisations all over Africa and India. Ireland by the 1840s, after years of British rule involving now-familiar hideous destructions – smashing the locals, stealing the resources, suppressing the language, culture and customs, crushing local industry, grabbing great swathes of land from the 'natives' and settling them with their own colonisers and/or soldiers loyal to the crown, etc. – was in a perilously unbalanced state, with governance from London doled out by privileged apparatchiks and a compliant Anglo-Irish aristocracy, with hundreds of thousands of native Irish subsisting in tiny mud cabins, on tiny smallholdings, entirely dependent on potatoes for their food.

When the potato crop failed due to a fungal blight in

1845, catastrophe swooped in. Subsequent failures of the crop in the following years compounded the misery.

Shockingly, as the people starved in their hundreds of thousands, ships loaded to the gunwales with corn and cattle sailed out of Irish ports for England. In 1847, one of the worst famine years, 630,538 cows, calves, sheep and pigs were exported to the UK, along with 146,000 tons of grain.[1]

As the people died, the big landlords, mainly Anglo-Irish, were given British government legal backing to 'clear' their estates, 'legally' demolishing whole villages, dumping thousands of paupered and destitute people into workhouses, into ditches by the roadside, or onto 'coffin ships' bound for Canada, Liverpool and New York. Fever, dysentery, cholera – and despair – spread like wildfire.

In 1848 *The London Illustrated News* reported:

> Calmly and quietly from Westminster itself did the decree go forth which has made the temporary but terrible visitation of a potato rot the means of exterminating, through the slow process of disease and houseless starvation, nearly half of the Irish.[2]

As Republican hero John Mitchel wrote at the time, 'The Almighty sent the blight but the British created the Famine.'[3]

---

1   Tóibín, Colm and Ferriter, Diarmaid, *The Irish Famine: A Documentary* (St Martin's Press, London, 2001) pp. 183–4.
2   *Illustrated London News*, 15 December 1849.
3   Tóibín and Ferriter (2001), p. 188.

And, just as the men who created the bank crash in 2007 fingered those on social welfare, much of the contemporary narrative around the famine blamed the 'licentiousness' of the ordinary people. It was their 'feckless' way of life, their 'laziness' that was at the root of the disaster. The famine was the 'hand of God'.

'The great evil with which we have to contend', wrote Sir Charles Trevelyan, the dude in charge of famine relief, 'is not the physical evil of the famine, but the moral evil of the selfish, perverse and turbulent character of the people.'[4]

Take, for example, the Earl of Middleton's rent book for 1847:

> No. 368. Received notice to quit.
>
> No. 369. Two of the tenants sent to Canada. Their portion of arrear will be lost.
>
> No. 370. Tenant dead; notice to quit given to widow.
>
> No. 372. Tenant removed.
>
> No. 373. Arrear lost. Tenant sent to Canada.
>
> Nos 375, 376, 377. Notices to quit.
>
> No. 379. Arrear lost. Tenant sent to Canada.
>
> No. 380. Notice to quit.
>
> No. 381. Arrear lost; tenant sent to Canada.

---

4   *Ibid.*

No. 382 and 384. Notices to quit.

No. 386. To be removed by ejectment.

No. 387. Arrear lost. Tenant sent to Canada.

Nos 390 and 391. Notices to quit.

No. 395. Arrear lost. Tenant removed.

No. 396. Tenant dead. Notice to quit given to widow.

No. 397. Arrear lost; tenant and family sent to Canada.[5]

A bald catalogue hiding so much horror.

The famine lasted from 1845 to 1849; when it was over, 1,622,739 native Irish had died of starvation or fever, or had fled.

A pre-famine population of eight-plus million collapsed ever downwards; by 1926 it was 2.97 million. Even today it is just over 4 million, making Ireland *the only country in the world that has a lower population now than it did in 1845.*

Truly the famine was a blow from which the country has never truly recovered.

Of course in the midst of war, famine and disaster there's always an opportunity. The people who spotted the opportunity, who rushed in to fill the power vacuum the famine left behind, were the Catholic Church and the 'tenant' or bigger farmers. The Church's foot soldiers were the children of the tenant farmers, as these farmers were the

---

5   *Ibid.*

only people who could afford to send their sons to Maynooth College to study for the priesthood. As Goretti Horgan writes in her paper 'Changing Women's Lives in Ireland', 'The Church was ... the large tenant farmer class at prayer.'[6]

The native Irish tenant farmers, often agents for land-lords and 'gombeen men' or moneylenders, believed that farms must be consolidated and never divided up as they had been in pre-famine days when each child got married. From now on the farm must be left to one son only, the remainder of the sons and daughters forced to live in 'permanent celi-bacy', to emigrate, or to enter 'Holy Orders', the priesthood or the nunnery.

In 1841 only 18 per cent of farms in Ireland were greater than fifteen acres. By 1891 more than 58 per cent were.

Before the famine the ratio of priests to people was 1 to 3,023. By 1911 it was 1 to 210. Convents, virtually non-existent before the 1840s, now numbered 360. The Virgin Mary – an icon stripped of sexuality and power, dressed in pastels, eyes cast down – was installed as the symbol of Irish womanhood: 'passive, virginal, pious, humble' with, crucially, 'an unlimited capacity to endure suffering'.[7]

Enforced celibacy dovetailed neatly with the Church's

6   Horgan, Goretti, 'Changing Women's Lives in Ireland', *Internation-al Socialism* (Summer 2002), https://www.marxists.org/history/etol/newspape/isj2/2001/isj2-091/horgan.htm.

7   Inglis, Tom, 'Origins and Legacies of Irish Prudery: Sexuality and Social Control in Modern Ireland', https://researchrepository.ucd.ie/handle/10197/5112.

ideology, providing 'the ideological basis for the sexual repression'.[8]

With the Gaelic-speaking small farm families wiped out, the Church and the 'respectable' tenant farmers were now to be entrusted with reconstructing a new and 'holy' Ireland. These two male groupings, with their primitive, misogynistic and conservative ideologies, began to shape Ireland and, most detrimentally, the lives of Irish women.

Still the new practices – puritanism and celibacy – went so violently against human nature that massive, ongoing reinforcements, punishments and shamings were necessary. How were normal people made to change practices they'd lived by for years? To quote Goretti Horgan again, 'Carrying on "normal life" after the famine was impossible.'[9]

Under respectability's rule a new paradigm of godliness, celibacy and sexual repression was held up for all to aspire to, with, conveniently for the Church, a cowed and frightened congregation at its command. A moral dictatorship was entrenched, with the Church in charge in the public sphere and mothers within the home charged with enforcing diktats that eschewed pleasure and sexuality, replacing them with shame, repression, guilt and fear.

A culture of silence, secrecy and hypocrisy ensued.

The enmeshment of many people in Ireland with

---

8   Horgan, 'Changing Women's Lives in Ireland', https://www.marxists.
     org/history/etol/newspape/isj2/2001/isj2-091/horgan.htm.
9   *Ibid.*

Catholicism can be linked to colonialism and the brutal suppression of religious expression. During penal times the priest was seen as the friend of the ordinary people. Catholic Emancipation (1829) had allowed some limited freedoms, but it was after the famine, more crucially, that the Church began to establish itself as a central power, 'above' the people.

In the late 1800s a deal was struck with the Irish Parliamentary Party under an aristocratic Protestant, Charles Stewart Parnell, who at the time, ironically, was involved in a passionate 'adulterous' love affair. He promised the Catholic Church control over public morality, health and education if they supported the nationalist cause, thereby consolidating the Church's pivotal position within Irish society, inside the body politic.

From the famine, as from all catastrophes, so much damage flowed.

UPPITY WOMEN

It wasn't until the suffrage movements at the turn of the century, with agitation for freedom for women as part of the nationalist struggle here, that participation by women in public life and campaigning for rights for women got going. Many of the more famous 'sisters' who took part in the struggle for independence – Countess Markievicz, Maud Gonne MacBride, Hanna Sheehy Skeffington, Mary MacSwiney, Margaret Skinnider, Elizabeth O'Farrell, Julia Grenan and Kathleen Lynn, to name just a few – were often a good deal more militant than the men.

Tragically, after the 1916 Rising, the War of Independence and the Civil War, with most of the poets, visionaries, communists, republicans and socialists executed, exiled or imprisoned, the revolutionary dreams of 1916 were shelved and Ireland shaped into a petit bourgeois, patriarchal autocracy. 'A Catholic country for a Catholic people' to quote President Éamon de Valera. Or, as writer Seán O'Faoláin put it: 'a dreary Eden'.

The high ideals of liberty, fraternity and equality between men and women espoused by the revolutionaries were forgotten. The 'uppity' women who'd fought and campaigned alongside the men in their thousands, who'd fought, trained Volunteers, hidden guns, carried messages and hidden men on the run, were shoved back into their drawing rooms and kitchens. Or forced, in disgust, to emigrate.

Countess Markievicz was made a government minister, but she didn't last long, her health destroyed by hunger strikes and years in prison. Having literally given her life for 'the cause', she died a pauper in the public ward of a Dublin hospital, the government refusing to give her the State funeral she deserved. Still, the countess got the last word: Dublin's poor lined the streets in their thousands to say their goodbyes. And the government looked like the asshats they were.

As if by dark magic, after all the fighting and bloodshed, the gombeen men and the Church once more came centre stage. As historian Brian Heffernan wrote in *Freedom and the Fifth Commandment*, 'for the conservatives, the foundation of the Irish Free State in 1922 was equivalent to the reaching of dry ground again'.[1] While the gombeen men took care of 'business' (politics, commerce, sport, landlordism), the Catholic hierarchy, as promised, ran schools, universities, hospitals, mental institutions, penitentiaries, industrial schools, and the infamous Mother and Baby Homes and Magdalene Laundries, with, of course, special opprobrium doled out for 'fallen' women. Fr James Cassidy, writing in 1922 in *The Women of the Gael*, opined:

---

1   *The Irish Times*, 9 January 2016, https://www.irishtimes.com/culture/books/freedom-and-the-fifth-commandment-by-brian-heffernan-raising-holy-hell-1.2489661.

In Ireland – whenever a child is born out of wedlock, so shocked is the public sense by the very unusual occurrence, that it brands it with irreparable stigma, and, to a large extent, excommunicates the woman guilty of the crime.[2]

This dovetailed nicely with a 1927 government report stating: 'The illegitimate child, being the proof of the mother's shame, is, in most cases, sought to be hidden at all costs.'[3]

That misogynistic, anti-woman, anti-child, patriarchal pattern held for decades: with a few outstanding exceptions, gombeen men and politicians, educated by Catholic brothers, nuns and priests, implemented the Church's diktats, often without enforcement of any kind being necessary.

Yes sir. No sir. Three bags full sir.

A dreary and patriarchal Eden indeed.

Let's face it – the gombeen men never were feminists. They never had an interest in liberating women from the kitchen. They wanted to keep them in there, cooking up big steak dinners for when they got back from a hard day's grafting, backslapping and the handing out of brown envelopes. Their objective was to keep power and respectability for themselves.

---

2   Smith, James M., 'The politics of sexual knowledge: the origins of Ireland's Containment Culture and the Carrigan Report (1931)', *Journal of the History of Sexuality* (1 April 2004), https://www2.bc.edu/james-smith-2/Politicsofsexualknowledge.pdf.
3   https://www.oireachtas.ie/en/debates/debate/dail/1934-02-07/38/.

The Catholic Church never was, and definitely is not now, feminist. In fact, it's so not feminist it would rather die than let women into positions of power – which, ironically, is exactly what's happening.

THE ARCHBISHOP AND TAMPAX

The Ireland that Bridget Cleary lived in and was murdered in had all but disappeared by the time Irish independence arrived. In the intervening fifty-plus years, British rule over Ireland had finally been broken and 'modern life' more or less arrived; its spread over urban and rural life was uneven but the faeries were gone. Still, in the post-independence 'dreary Eden' fabricated by Church and State, the Church's power over governments and women's lives remained extraordinarily strong. Like many post-colonial societies, we'd swapped one set of dictatorial rulers for another.

The Church's unchallenged power threw up some very weird situations. Founding father Éamon de Valera and Archbishop John McQuaid, 'the J. Edgar Hoover of the Catholic Church', collaborated on the drafting of the 1937 Constitution and it was their puritanical vision that coloured every aspect of Irish law and life. Writing in *The Irish Times* on 7 April 2003, John Cooney, McQuaid's biographer, emphasised how widely McQuaid's writ ran:

> [A] control freak, McQuaid mobilised government departments, Dublin Corporation, and the medical, legal and teaching professions to defend 'Catholic Ireland' from the liberal wiles of *The Irish Times*, Trinity College, and the Communist Party.

Between the two of them, and their willing enforcers, we had our very own Taliban.

Not only was the Church's obsession with women's sexuality unchallenged by the State, it was enforced by it. Take the chillingly named 'Catholic Rescue Society', which boasted a 98 per cent success rate in tracking down pregnant girls. Founded in 1913, initially to help children of workers of the 1913 Lockout, the Catholic Rescue Society morphed into something much darker post-independence, where sexual behaviour and its regulation were now the Church's obsessions. The (lay) Catholic Rescue Society became one of the chief enforcers of those obsessions.

Tipped off by a nasty neighbour, or the local priest, pregnant girls were ruthlessly hunted in their homes, or to where they had fled – to bedsits in Dublin, or to aunts or sisters in England, and brought back to Ireland, back to often lifelong incarceration in a Magdalene Laundry or a Mother and Baby Home. Not only did the State not protect these girls and women, it actually paid the Church to imprison and exploit them. As Lorraine Grimes of Warwick University points out, 'institutionalism was the only form of social care'.[1]

The Catholic Church's writ, vigorously implemented by

---

1 Grimes, Lorraine, '"They Go to England to Preserve their Secret": The Emigration and Assistance of the Irish Unmarried Mother in Britain 1926–1952', *Retrospectives*, Vol. 5, Issue 1 (Warwick University, Warwick, 2016), p. 51.

the Catholic Rescue Society, went so far as to remove babies from Protestant families into which they'd been adopted in England and bring them back to institutions in Ireland and into the awful 'architecture of containment' from which many never reappeared, going, undocumented, from Mother and Baby Home to Industrial School to Magdalene Laundry to an unmarked grave.[2] As Diarmaid Ferriter noted drily in *The Transformation of Ireland*:

> It was ironic that a society which placed such a premium on the family and the home environment was still prepared to incarcerate children in institutions where childhood was all but non-existent, while legal adoption continued to be resisted on the grounds that it would threaten the religious welfare of children.[3]

It was a horrible, misshapen disaster that has affected us all, heaping shame and guilt on everyone, particularly, of course, on girls and women. So much shame and guilt that it turned people against each other.

After years of colonisation, of patriarchy and Catholicism, we had become, as Nell McCafferty called it, 'Damaged Cowboys' (expanding and making local Annie Proulx's riff), unloved, unable to love:

---

2   *Ibid.*, p. 54.
3   Ferriter, Diarmaid, *The Transformation of Ireland* (Profile Books, London, 2004) p. 392.

taking unloving bites out of each other in the name of the self-proclaimed holy men, who effectively abolished God and imposed their own, wretched manmade rules on our behaviour, aided and abetted by the men of medicine and the law.[4]

We were Damaged Cowboys all. Damaged by the Catholic Church, a damage cemented by government after government that slavishly followed every creepy twist or turn boiling up in the strange minds of the Church 'Fathers'.

In a fascinating piece for *History Ireland*, writer Margaret Ó hÓgartaigh gives an insight into how deeply obsessed with women's bodies the hierarchy was, and how instantly these obsessions became law. All these princes of the Church had to do was write to the relevant minister, or private secretary, saying they didn't like this or that, and this or that, which usually had to do with matters sexual, was instantly banned.[5]

Take, for instance, some of Archbishop McQuaid's weird fixations on women playing sport alongside men. 'Mixed athletics and all cognate immodesties are abuses that right-minded people reprobate, wherever and whenever they exist,' he thundered wordily. The Christian Brothers instantly

---

4   McCafferty, Nell, *A Woman to Blame: the Kerry Babies Case* (Cork University Press, Cork, 2010) , p. xxvi.
5   Ó hÓgartaigh, Margaret, 'Internal Tamponage, Hockey Parturition and Mixed Athletics', *History Ireland*, Issue 6, Vol. 15 (November–December 2007): https://www.historyireland.com/20th-century-contemporary-history/internal-tamponage-hockey-parturition-and-mixed-athletics/.

backed him wholeheartedly in his 'splendid protest' and the GAA dutifully waded in, with a Dr Magnier in Cork saying '"people of influence" asked that women not be allowed to play at Croke Park', pointing out that from the 'moral point of view it was absolutely wrong to be running young men and women in the same field in the same garb now effected for these events'.[6]

Then it was Tampax. Yes, Tampax. One of Ireland's highest ranking celibates demanded tampons be banned in case us ladies derived sexual pleasure from them, or *mirabile dictu*, that they might secretly be contraceptives. At a time when civil servants responding to the archbishop signed off as: 'Your loyal, humble and most obedient servant', McQuaid wrote to the parliamentary secretary to the minister for health, saying he had explained to his fellow bishops:

> very fully the evidence concerning the use of internal sanitary tampons, in particular, that called Tampax. On the medical evidence made available, the bishops very strongly disapproved of the use of these appliances, more particularly in the case of unmarried persons.[7]

In 1947 tampons were duly banned by the government of Ireland.

---

6   *Ibid.*
7   *Ibid.*

As late as the 1960s the archbishop was concerning himself with 'unnatural pleasures' associated with female gymnastics, especially the pommel horse.

The *pommel* horse.

It's horrible to think back on all the suffering that the nonsensical clerical censoring of pleasure of any kind caused people. Particularly so in working-class and rural communities, where any aberration from the norm by a girl or a woman could bring instant, often violent, punishment.

SEX, LONDON
AND THE IWLM

SECTION III

LONDON AND THE 1960S

After years in the convent boarding school, I was green as a cabbage. Still, I leapt into miniskirts, knee-high boots and gigantic shades, and made for the bright lights of London, heart on my sleeve, pounding. Full of beans and cheerfully oblivious to the machinations of the archbishop, London beckoned. It was 1965. Big Sis, already there, got me a job as a secretary in the fledgling Amnesty International. She was secretary to its (wonderful) barrister founder, Peter Benenson. Amnesty's president, Seán MacBride, leaking legendary exotic vibes, visited regularly, pronouncing Big Sis's legs 'ze most bew-ti-full I have ever seen'.

I shared a tiny bedroom with sis in a flat in Queensgate. Underneath my bed, vacated for me by Hattie Waugh, daughter of Evelyn, was a fantastic crush of taffeta, silk and satin, or all of Hattie's debs dresses, worn once then shoved into oblivion.

Big Sis also got me a night job as a 'hat check' girl at Parkes restaurant in Beauchamp Place, Knightsbridge, then *the* nobby eatery of the day. Run by working-class Liverpudlian Tom Benson, it nightly hosted the in-crowd. Down the tiny dark stairwell came Margot Fonteyn, Rudolf Nureyev, Jean Shrimpton, David Bailey, Terence Donovan, Terence Stamp, Twiggy, The Beatles and The Rolling Stones!

As we reeled under the weight of furs and capes and hats and canes, our job was to remember exactly which velvet opera cloak, mink or floor-length black leather belonged to who and have it ready and waiting, *prontissimo!*, when the glitterati emerged after the delights of Tom's fabulous cooking.

I was busy having a glorious time, grabbing every opportunity to liberate myself from the past.

Next I got a job as a secretary in the BBC and a side hustle as a 'runner' in BBC Television Centre, literally running from the fifth floor down to the studios to bring a news update or a sandwich to Richard Dimbleby or Robin Day on set.

On Saturdays, Hattie introduced me to the Kings Road and South Kensington, to Mary Quant, Lord Kitchener's and Biba. Oh Biba! Emporium extraordinaire with its velvet pants, jackets with sleeves buttoned to the elbow, purple canvas boots buttoned to the knee, floor-length jersey dresses, huge felt hats and pink feather boas.

Biba's creator, Barbara Hulanicki, on TV said she wanted it to be a place where girls could 'develop their personalities' in a 'make-believe atmosphere'. Develop our personalities? A make-believe atmosphere? Had no one told her that taking pleasure in life was wrong? That self-love was no love, as the nuns loved to say?

Apparently not. Heaven had arrived on earth. London was a playground of earthly pleasures.

REALLY CHRISTINE KEELER

Not that England didn't have issues with pleasure and pleasure-loving women during that period. In 1963 the newspapers thought they had died and gone to heaven when the Christine Keeler story broke in London – a torrid tale peopled with toffs, 'party girls' and Reds not just under the bed but in the bed too.

Poster child of the 'Swinging Sixties', Christine Keeler's bio as that of a 'good-time girl' who brought down the Tory government by having an affair with the minister for war, John Profumo, while having it off with a Soviet naval attaché at the same time, was, in reality, more complicated.

She was just a teenager from a deprived, dysfunctional background when she ran away to 'Swinging London', her only currency her looks. Her mother was abandoned by her own mother, and Keeler's father, from the nearby RAF base, abandoned them both. Christine was emotionally abused by her mother – she was taken out of her home as a nine-year-old suffering from malnutrition – then sexually abused by her stepfather from the age of twelve. She became pregnant at seventeen, but her baby was born prematurely as a result of a botched abortion with a pen, and died six days later, so her life was anything but a party.

When Keeler came to prominence in the 1960s,

repression and hypocrisy still ruled in public life; in private, the ruling Tory classes were embracing the parallel world of sexual liberation and the 'Swinging Sixties' with gusto. 'Sexy' parties were all the go.

There was, as yet, no Women's Movement, no MeToo, no one standing up for eighteen- and nineteen-year-old girls from working-class backgrounds in the 'sex industry'. Pretty, uneducated and innocent, they were gorgeous chicks to be fed to the circling male hawks. Who cared if their feathers were torn off? Who cared what became of them when their prettiness faded? They were 'party girls', 'women of easy virtue', 'prostitutes' – the lowest of the low. Compared to the big rich males who ogled them on stage and had sex with them at parties, they were barely considered human. Certainly not worthy of compassion of any kind.

A fragile, nervy beauty, Keeler's 'currency' brought her to the attention of Dr Stephen Ward, an osteopath who manipulated the twisted spines and limbs of the rich and famous, and drew their portraits. Clients included members of the royal family, Sir Winston Churchill, Paul Getty, Douglas Fairbanks Junior and Elizabeth Taylor.

Ward had been gifted (rent was £1 a year) a gate lodge on the Cliveden Estate, the palatial home on the Thames of the hugely wealthy and influential Astor family, and he spent most weekends there bringing down 'party girls' from the London scene for the toffs. You give me access to your fabulous gaff and aristo scene for next to nothing, and I'll give you party girls. Not exactly PC. It was at the swimming pool in Cliveden that John Profumo, then minister for war, first spotted the young Christine swimming naked in the moonlight.

At the time, unbeknownst to Profumo, and presumably to Christine, Stephen Ward had been encouraged to compromise Eugene Ivanov, a naval attaché at the Soviet embassy.

According to the makers of the 1989 film *Scandal*, Ward, with his unparalleled access to the elite crowd, was put together with Ivanov by the then editor of *The Daily Telegraph*, Colin Coote, an ex-army man. Ward was encouraged to give Ivanov 'anything he wants'. Before you could say sex, lies and videotape, Ivanov was being whirled down to Cliveden and exposed to the earthly pleasures there on tap, particularly the beautiful eighteen-year-old Ms Keeler.

It was a honey trap, with Christine as the honey and MI5 hoping to trap Ivanov, out him as a spy and force him to defect to their side; unfortunately, greedy Mr Profumo, minister for war, took the honey first.

The following week the minister for war's Rolls Royce drew up outside Stephen Ward's Marylebone flat – where Keeler was now living – to take her on a tour of the great buildings of parliament. He was nice, she told Ward afterwards, kind. Soon, however, he was more than 'kind' and was having a full-blown affair with a girl young enough to be his daughter, except of course no daughter of his would have worked in 'cabaret' or been a 'party girl'. Ward had meanwhile ensured that Ivanov was also exposed to Ms Keeler's charms and, hey presto, Ivanov fell.

The whole sorry fandango only came to light when a jealous ex-lover turned up at Stephen Ward's flat shouting and firing off shots. Residents were appalled. The police were called. Ward, 'the only man I ever really loved', turned on Keeler, saying enough was enough; the party was over. She had to get out as she had 'gone too far'.

Keeler lost her friend, the flat she and her friend Mandy Rice Davies lived in with Ward, plus her connection to the high life. She and Rice Davies turned to the press. In return for money, they would tell their sensational story of high life with the high enders.

The Establishment went quietly apeshit. This was the middle of the Cold War, and the Americans, already appalled at security breaches in upper-crust English circles, smelled blood. John Profumo at first denied all knowledge of the affair: 'I never had sex with that woman.' Sorry, that was another leading male politician with another vulnerable young girl, wasn't it? Anyhow, after mucho bluster, Profumo fessed up, then resigned. Prime Minister Macmillan resigned. The government fell.

Then there was that photo: the Arne Jacobson designer chair, that beautiful naked young woman.

The world was agog.

'What the hell is going on in this country?' shouted the *Daily Mirror*.

First and foremost scapegoats had to be found: 'flâneur' Stephen Ward would do nicely. He was arrested and put on trial for 'living off immoral earnings', though both Christine Keeler and Mandy Rice Davies later said he had been more likely to give them money than the other way round. The police managed to drum up 157 witnesses, many of whom Ward said he didn't even know, with Christine and Mandy the trial stars. They were clickbait for the world's media, having their hair done in Vidal Sassoon's every morning, rocking up to court in taxis looking like film stars. They enjoyed the notoriety, hoping a short sojourn in jail for Ward would wake him up and put them in the money – the papers now finally legally able to print the scandalous stuff they were spilling. Meanwhile all of Ward's toff chums quietly abandoned him.

That the truth would come out – that Ward was working for MI5, that he had the low-down on virtually everyone high up – was not to be contemplated. A 'hanging' judge was appointed, the sex angle was played up, and day after day Stephen Ward's name and reputation were mired. He was 'a communist sympathiser', 'a master spy', a 'ponce', 'filth'. The day before judgment was due, Ward took an overdose. In a letter to a friend he wrote:

> It is not only fear, it is a wish not to let them get me. I would rather get myself. I do hope I have not let people down too much. I tried to do my stuff but after Marshall's summing-up,

I've given up all hope.[1]

Xan Brooks, writing in *The Guardian* on the eve of the Andrew Lloyd Webber musical about the whole affair, said:

> The broadcaster Tom Mangold, then working as a news-paper reporter, visited Ward on the night of his overdose. He watched as the man wrote out his suicide notes and prepared for the end. Mangold wanted to stay and help out if he could. But his marriage was in freefall and he had to go home.[2]

Ward died in hospital three days later. At the cremation, Kenneth Tynan, the legendary drama critic, sent a wreath with a card that read: 'Stephen Ward – Victim of Hypocrisy'.

When Christine ran from the courtroom, crying, the following morning, upon hearing the news, she was mobbed, the car taking her away thronged by women bashing the windows yelling, 'Witch! Witch!'

At first Keeler managed to live reasonably well, but after a while nobody cared if it was a spy scandal or a sex scandal. The case was closed, Ward was dead, and Christine Keeler was stranded. In a painful interview with Sue Lawley of the BBC after the premiere of *Scandal*, the 1989 film of her story, she was asked about her motives for endorsing it.

---

1   *The Guardian*, 5 December 2017.
2   *The Guardian*, 11 December 2013.

Hadn't John Profumo and his wife suffered enough? Wasn't bringing it all out into the open again 'rubbing his nose in it', asked Sue Lawley, her own BBC nose twitching with distaste.

John Profumo! An extremely wealthy man, married to an extremely wealthy wife, sainted by the Establishment for a few week's work he did among London's East End poor. This man had apparently 'suffered' more than the nineteen-year-old girl caught up in a ferocious world she had virtually no agency in, apart from her looks; who was brutally discarded, smeared as a 'prostitute', a 'fortune hunter', a 'courter of fame' when that ferocious world saw its own interests threatened.

Please.

When Profumo died in 2006, *The Telegraph* called him 'a man who made one terrible mistake but sought his own redemption in a way which has no precedent in public life either before or since'.

Excuse me while I die laughing.

Christine Keeler lived on. She had two brief marriages and two sons. The second, Seymour Platt, lives in Ireland. He spoke up for his departed mum the week after her death in 2017, saying she was a devoted, loving mother. 'She was a good, decent person and got a very unfair label that was hard for her to live with.' She was 'feisty', he said, 'she would never shy away from a fight. She had a terrific sense of fairness. She would stand up against anybody she thought was doing the wrong thing.'[3]

Christine lived out her days in poverty in a tower block in World's End and later in sheltered accommodation, the tabloids pouncing every so often to take ghastly photos of the 'Look how Christine Keeler has Deteriorated' variety.

She did everything she could to clear her name – giving interviews, writing books, participating in documentary projects about her life. In *Secrets and Lies*, her 2012 autobiography, some pages at the very end give an inkling of what she was up against: sentence after sentence blacked out. To this day the transcript of her testimony at Stephen Ward's trial hasn't been made public. Nor has that of Stephen Ward. In an interview in the 1990s, she said: 'I wish that I had been older then, so I could have been able to answer, to speak up for myself. And for Stephen.'[4]

Amanda Coe, putting together a documentary about her story for the BBC, said that Keeler was adamant that she didn't want to be portrayed as a victim. How brave! Particularly since the truth is the opposite: she was a beautiful, and abused, victim of the patriarchy almost from the day she was born. These days Keeler would be a heroine of MeToo. Feminist artist Caroline Coon believes Keeler was a young, working-class girl who got scapegoated, 'criminally'.[5]

Oh yes, the 1960s weren't all fun and games.

3   *The Guardian*, 5 December 2017.
4   *Evening Standard*, 6 December 2017.
5   *The Guardian*, 18 February 2001.

DAD'S DEATH

The night before Dad's death I was in London, sitting on a round velvet stool at a grand piano, nearby eighteen-foot-high Georgian windows looking out onto a sleeping South Ken. It was 3 a.m. and I was writing Dad a letter. Coming clean. Telling him that far from living a healthy, happy, jolly-young-girl life in London, enjoying my job, lapping up the culture, sharing jolly japes with Big Sis and Hattie as I had pretended to be doing, I was actually living with an older married man, a friend of Big Sis – the very same man I had promised Dad on my life's blood I would never even think about, or ever see, ever ever *ever* again.

Now this man's wife had gone off with his 'best' friend, so he was technically free, and definitely eager. The first night we hopped into bed, over six months earlier, Big Sis had invited me to London for a weekend break after I, back living in Dublin, had split up with a boyfriend. He had just flown in from Rome where he and a friend had comprehensively trashed a hotel room after hearing the news of his wife's jumping ship. In my innocence – still a teenager – I thought it incredibly romantic and Rolling Stones-ish. He looked like Sean Connery and, unfortunately, had a reputation to match. He was cleverer and sexier and more worldly than anyone I'd ever met – previous boyfriends seemed like uncooked turnips in comparison. He was also ten years older than me.

As you can imagine, when Big Sis spilled the beans, Dad and Mum were seriously horrified. What the *hell*, Rosita? Dad threatened to make me a ward of court. Mum wouldn't talk to me. No one in the family would talk to me. Eventually I promised Dad I wouldn't ever see him again. But, instead, I had simply returned to London, met up with him on my first night there, and moved in.

Now, suddenly, I had decided to come clean, tell Dad the truth and ask for forgiveness.

Letter completed, I pulled it out of my little green portable Olivetti, folded it into an envelope and climbed back up the stairs (to the married man in question) and to bed.

The phone rang downstairs just after 7.30 a.m. It was Big Sis's husband ringing from Ireland. She and he and their newborn were visiting home.

'There's bad news.'

'Oh.'

'Your father died this morning.'

There was running up three flights of stairs, screaming, the walls of the house disappearing, the stairs seeming to climb through rushing air, the house falling away, the world falling away, the screams, my screams, coming from thousands of miles away. My inamorato sitting up in bed – 'Oh fuck.'

On the plane home there was no plane, there were no

sounds, there was no seat, there were no clouds packed like dirty cotton wool beneath the outstretched metal arms, there was no whiskey. At the house, Mum opened the front door, her eyes bright with tears. 'Come in, Pet.' Death had smashed her carapace clean off. I felt suddenly afraid. Mum looked so alive, so terrifyingly vulnerable.

Dad's death changed everything. Each of us was now separately imprisoned in the magnesium flash of shock. The older ones arranged everything – funeral, obituaries, mass, visits. Mum sat in the drawing room in her good clothes – bright, glass-like, bereft.

Dad's body lay in my brother's room at the top of the house, a scarecrow tricked out by undertakers to fake aliveness. Sand-coloured skin drawn tight over high wide forehead, high cheekbones, carved jaw. He looked like a concentration-camp inmate who hadn't made it.

That evening, standing at the cooker, I made omelette after omelette, the blue-and-yellow gas flames rushing up the sides of the pan, me calling out, 'How many to go?' while looking over my shoulder at my family, crowded together at the old kitchen table. Mum, red stains high in each cheek, sat at the top of the table as if she were still Mum, as if we were still children, as if as long as I kept the big hearty Spanish omelettes coming, and the plates were passed hand to hand, and the salt was passed across the table, and the pepper was sent from the top of the table to the bottom, and more toast was rammed into the toaster, then the horror that had struck the house would retreat. It would all turn out to be a ghastly nightmare, and any minute Dad – and safety and love – would walk back in the door, saying, 'Hello there my great big nest of hooley birds.'

For years afterwards I had nightmares. Guilt at having deceived Dad. The letter of confession I'd written the night before his death was still on top of the piano in the big house in London when I got back, Dad left behind, buried in a great lumpy graveyard in Dublin.

A strange thing happened at Dad's funeral. Just as the terrible sarcophagus was leaving the church, my brother's then girlfriend came up, linked my arm and said she and I were going to have a drink. It seemed so strange. Why? I was in such shock I went along. Next thing we were drinking brandies in the lounge of the Gresham Hotel.

It was only later that I discovered the older ones in the family had decided that I should not be allowed to go to the graveside. That I had been too upset at seeing Dad dead. Upset? I thought I would lose my mind seeing him laid out there on the bed like a Belsen scarecrow. Dead. *Dad*?

The last few years for Mum and Dad had been awful. Dad's health was going downhill, each day a struggle. He set off to his work a ghost inside his suit, hated by his wife who could not, would not, forgive him for abandoning her on the day of my little sister's death. At night, on my visits home, I could hear him, lying in bed, coughing, coughing, while Mum sat alone in the drawing room, knitting, the little black-and-white television hissing in the far corner, her Jack Russell at her feet.

I'm ashamed to say it, but mostly we had sided with Dad. Mum was so frozen and so angry, so profoundly depressed, I don't remember any of us even trying to understand how she felt, or why she felt how she did. It was just Mum hating Dad. Us hating Mum for hating Dad. Dad dying of sadness but none of us able to talk about why things were so fucked up.

There was no counselling. No outside help. You made your bed. You lay in it.

It took me twenty years to cry properly for him. And for Mum.

AFTER

Mum and Dad were hopeless, really. They should have swapped roles. Mum should have had control of finances and Dad been the carer. He was a natural – gentle, empathetic, intelligent, always thinking up wonderful projects for us children to get involved in. Children's parties were legendary affairs at our house; at one, Dad devised a pirate ship out of old scrap and thrillingly burnt it at the end of the party. Posh upper-middle-class mummies and daddies came to collect their little darlings, who now looked like something off the set of *Lord of the Flies* – covered in water, blackened with soot, posh clothes in flitters, all gathered around Dad, who was also wet and blackened, the kids squealing and yelling like the little savages young children really are. Upstairs, Mum poured sherry in the drawing room.

Mum was not a natural carer. She was high wire. Ambitious. Snappy. Before marriage she had loved hunting, point-to-points, parties, skiing, travelling, reading, fast cars, and handsome, intelligent men. Was the universe taking the piss when it landed her with nine children and a super-delicate husband whose health kept breaking down? A world where money was always scarce? A world in which she eventually became the baddie, the one who scolded, punished, chastised? The one who was so alone?

After Dad's death we left her, one by one. Hurrying off to jobs, boyfriends and universities. At first, charged with post-death energy, she began renovating the house. The drawing room was repapered. Floor-length velvet curtains were ordered. The staircase and its four landings were painted top to bottom in glorious white gloss.

The older ones didn't approve. They said she was 'manic', that she was spending too much money. That she was being extravagant. Maybe, but she seemed alive, doing stuff; not the frozen simulacrum she had been since Cathy's death. Surely this was a good thing?

Gradually, as loneliness – that hideous mould that creeps in and smothers everything – took over, she sank back into her frozen state. The more withdrawn she became, the less we all visited. Guilt, and a kind of terror at witnessing what was happening, kept us away.

There was no sisterhood. No support for the matriarch. Zero female solidarity. We were Daddy's girls and that was that. Mum could sink or swim on her own.

Back home, on holiday, I was at one of my sisters' houses for a supper party. Mum was there. She got tipsy and retreated to a bedroom for a 'little lie-down'. Pretty tipsy myself, I found her lying on the bed in the dark, shoes still on, eyes enamelled with tears: 'You all loved your father more than me. You would all have preferred him to live and not me.' I swayed towards her, 'No Mum. No way!' But she was right. None of us really gave a damn.

Society didn't help much either. Mum learned the bitter lessons of widowhood in a patriarchal world – a woman no longer part of a couple is no longer a desirable guest. All of the 'friends' who'd attended Mum and Dad's drinks parties, dinner parties and children's parties mysteriously vanished. Invitations no longer appeared on the mantelpiece with their black embossed italic lettering, gold-leaf rims. Phone calls dried to a trickle. Weddings, christenings, engagement parties seemed to go along very well, thank you, without her. Money, which had always been tight, was now a tiny widow's pension. There were no more family holidays; Christmas was a ghastly charade. The little black-and-white TV was now Mum's only friend. That and her little dog Tinker.

ABORTION

Back in London I was just nineteen when I had my abortion. I didn't really want to have an abortion. Dad had just died. I was in shock and living with the taboo married man.

The first thing I remember is getting sick into the lavatory at seven in the morning. Not really sick, it was more just a yellow streak of bile. Prince Charming was not in the least amused. Bloody hell, you're pregnant. What? By this stage I was curled up on the manky double bed we shared, wishing he'd put his arms around me and say, 'There, there sweetness, everything's okay. Why don't I make you a cup of tea?'

Fresh from that Irish Catholic all-female convent boarding school, I was like, 'I'm *pregnant*?', while he was leafing frantically through his black notebook, looking for phone numbers. Two ex-girlfriends were whistled up, phone numbers were obtained, and next thing I knew I was on a bus and on the way to an obstetrician so posh he was called 'Mister', not 'Doctor', had a secretary who looked as if she had walked out of the pages of *Vogue*, and waiting rooms from an interiors' magazine. The doctor himself was cold. Contemptuous.

'I'll see you at eight tomorrow morning.'

'Tomorrow.'

'You do *want* this, don't you?'

Next it was off to a psychiatrist. His place was shambolic, with cats sprawled on top of sofas covered with books and magazines, and plants sprawling up not very clean windows.

'You are definitely suicidal?'

'Sorry, what?' I was busy stroking one of the cats.

'If I don't sign this form giving the go-ahead for the termination of your pregnancy you will be in danger of committing suicide.' He looked up, prompted, 'Yes?'

The penny dropped. 'Yes.'

Next thing it was 8 a.m. and I was standing outside the abortion clinic with my overnight bag. Alone. Buggery Prince Charming didn't even come with me to the door.

'You'll be fine.'

Now I felt frightened.

Inside I was ushered into a small ward. Undressed and shaved. The nurses, the orderlies, the receptionists were all polite, but coolly distant. This was a private abortion clinic and everyone knew what you were here for.

Right.

In the operating theatre the orderly was laughing like a drain: 'Here's one come in wiv her knickers on!'

Oh, if only the ground could have opened up and swallowed me. Actually, if only the ground could have opened up and swallowed him, the wanky little bastard.

Knickers off, my legs were hoisted up into steel stirrups and Dr Cold approached through swing doors, pulling on rubber gloves, as the anaesthetist, a kindly dude who told the wanky little orderly to shut his gob, counted me down: twenty-one, twenty, nineteen, eighteen, sev–

And I was gone.

When I woke up Prince Charming was at the end of the bed, looking at his watch.

'I have to go soon. Marie is meeting me for a drink.'

My insides felt as if they'd gone through twelve periods in a row.

'I need painkillers.'

'I'll tell the nurse on the way down,' says he and was gone.

Half an hour later a single Dispirin in a steel kidney dish arrived.

One.

I had a little weep.

***

Three weeks later, Prince Charming was gone. By some supposed miracle, he had been offered a post on the other side of the world. Couldn't wait. Running around the shops, buying new gear, notebooks, pens, briefcase, a wash bag. I was a horrible mess and was definitely not wanted on the new adventure.

I cried and cried and cried until my face resembled a bucket of wet laundry. I sat up all night, drinking whiskey, chain-smoking Gauloises and listening to Bob Dylan.

To be honest, I wasn't crying about the abortion. I was

crying about me. About the great lover I thought I had who'd turned out to be less responsive than a fridge. I was crying about my Prince Charming dreams and the brutal less-than-Prince-Charming reality.

I bought a huge navy sweater, and limped home to Ireland. I didn't take the sweater off for weeks.

'You're depressed,' said one of my big sisters.

'What?'

'You've been in that jumper for seven weeks now. What's wrong with you?'

I couldn't tell her about Prince Charming, or the abortion. In those far-off days we didn't talk about abortions. They were something men made you do. They were done in secret.

Susan Brownmiller, one of the great founding members of second-wave feminism, and the author of the ground-breaking analysis of rape *Against Our Will*, said that she had three (backstreet) abortions in New York and it was only at one of the early consciousness-raising sessions that she realised she'd never told anybody, not even her best friend, who was sitting beside her.

Looking back, I am so INCREDIBLY glad I was marched down the abortion corridor. Fresh from the virgin megastore that is a Catholic boarding school, I was about as capable of becoming a mother as a four-year-old. Sure, I could spout a bit of Latin, write a passable essay on Daniel O'Connell, read French, and fashion an apron from an old tablecloth, but making a lasting relationship with a man and giving birth to and raising a healthy, balanced child, children? Not a hope in hell.

Feminist Caitlin Moran wrote, during the abortion referendum here in Ireland, about the dangers of forcing inadequately prepared mothers to have babies; that what you end up with, what society ends up with, is a mess, or 'a mother who fails in mothering – who is traumatised, absent, ill or abused – [and] is apt to raise angry, traumatised children'.[1]

A traumatised nineteen-year-old in deep shock at her Dad's death with a dodgy Prince Charming not on side – I'm absolutely certain that, if I hadn't had an abortion, I would have been one of those mothers.

I'm so very, very glad I wasn't. I had seventeen more years of growing up to do before I even approached adequate mothering capabilities and had my own two beloved babes, now healthy, happy, loved and loving adults.

Just a few things on abortion here: of *course* I understand people's sensitivities about abortion. Nobody looks at their daughter and thinks, *Wow, I can't wait for her to have her first abortion*. But every woman in the world has to have the right to choose if she is going to go ahead with a pregnancy or not. The alternative is barbaric.

Unfortunately, if you were to believe the die-hard anti-abortionist lobby, you'd be forgiven for thinking abortions

---

1   *The Times*, 12 May 2018.

involve Darth Vader with a chainsaw astride the swollen belly of a twenty-something blonde trollop, snarfing cocktails and taking selfies while good old Darth rips a plump and dimpled two-year-old blond child from her womb before chucking it down the rubbish chute.

In the early days of second-wave feminism in New York, some of the more radical sisters offered free, non-medical, non-hospital-based, early term abortions to the sisterhood. Their kit? A cannula (or hollow tube) and a fridge motor. The point being that most abortions, or terminations of pregnancy, do not involve Darth Vader, chainsaws, dimpled two-year-olds or blonde trollops. They involve the removal of material that, yes, has the potential to be a human life, but at this stage of development can be sucked out through a tube from a woman WHO DOES NOT WANT TO BE PREGNANT.

In her testimony to a parliamentary committee in Dublin in November 2017, Dr Patricia Lohr, medical director of the British Pregnancy Advice Service (BPAS), said that 92 per cent of abortions in the UK the previous year were done at under thirteen weeks' gestation, and 81 per cent at under ten weeks'. Abortions after twenty weeks' gestation account for only 1 per cent of all abortions performed and usually involve teenage pregnancies where fear and lack of education prevented young girls accessing, and acting on, medical advice and help early.

Most abortions are carried out for women in their

twenties and thirties, mostly for women already in relation-ships, mostly already rearing families. Despite the alarm bells furiously rung by the pro-lifers, abortion rates remain largely stable across the UK, France and Sweden, where abortion is legal; abortion rates remain largely the same whether the procedure is legal or not. Women find a way.

Since time began women have shoved all and every kind of herb, potion and poison up their vaginas to try to control fertility. Following the 'witch burnings' of the Middle Ages, which wiped out the herbal wisdom of centuries, or 'Eve's Herbs', it wouldn't be until the late 1880s, when Annie Besant and Charles Bradlaugh argued it was 'more moral to prevent the conception of children, than, after they are born, to murder them by want of food, air and clothing' that the road to control for women opened up again.[2]

Sadly the knowledge of 'Eve's Herbs' doesn't seem to have been revived. Abortion these days is purely a chemical, or hospital, business.

Terrifyingly, even up to today, the Catholic Church – the largest provider of health care in the world – bans contraception and abortion, and even discourages the use of condoms. This has all led to disastrous consequences for women, particularly women in poorer countries. Well-off white women in the West can ignore the Church's 'abortion

---

2   Dinnage, Rosemary, *Annie Besant* (Penguin Books, London, 1986), p. 38.

brings instant excommunication' nonsense (and still go to church), but what of the millions of poor women worldwide?

The Guttmacher Institute believes proper birth control could prevent 52 million unintended pregnancies, 14 million unsafe abortions and 70,000 maternal deaths a year. A *year*.

'BIG TRINITY BLONDE'

In 1967 I landed a job in Dublin as a research assistant on *Seven Days*, a current affairs programme led by Lelia Doolan. Eoghan Harris interviewed me in the RTÉ canteen. He said they were looking for 'a big Trinity blonde'. (Definitely pre-PC days.) I wasn't that big. I wasn't a Trinity grad. I wasn't even that blonde. But being young and eager, I gladly accepted the tag.

Way for the Big Trinity Blonde!

Seven Days was wonderful. Every week the entire country waited to see which shyster, what corruption, we would expose next. We worked in two caravans parked outside the main RTÉ building. Lelia was definitely the boss, with John O'Donoghue, Brian Cleeve, Brian Farrell, Paddy Gallagher, David Thornley and Ted Nealon her knights in shining armour; Eoghan Harris her director; and me, coffee-girl extraordinaire and researcher.

I met many interesting, divisive figures.

One evening I collected Enoch Powell, the British Conservative MP famous for his 1968 'Rivers of Blood' speech about immigration, in which he warned that the 'tragic and intractable phenomenon which we watch with horror' in America (i.e. mass immigration) would soon unfold in the UK. His speech made him a national figure and got him sacked by Ted Heath from the Tory cabinet. I was sent to collect him from the airport and to take him to dinner in the Saddle Room of the Shelbourne, as they weren't ready for him back at Montrose. In the beautiful baroque glamour of the old Saddle Room, I sat opposite this strange, brilliant, bitter insect-man who, bafflingly, seemed entirely unimpressed by my miniskirted, twenty-something hoopla. He ordered prawns in garlic. Not to be outdone by the old bollix, I said I'd have the same and dutifully crunched my way through king prawns, shells and all, wondering why everyone raved about the damn things so much. Powell made no comment apart from one very briefly raised eyebrow. I don't think kindness, like pointing out gently that prawns were eaten with their shells off, was part of his make-up.

Sadly, after ten years on air, *Seven Days* was eventually muzzled. We had been the first current affairs programme to have politicians live on air for our features. A team of intelligent, educated, confident professionals led by a fearless woman, we were gleefully digging into every uncomfortable pile of hypocrisy we could find, and the politicos hated it. There were tumultuous meetings, but in the end 'the suits' won.

Some would argue RTÉ has never truly re-found its mojo. When I visited a couple of years ago with my son, Luke, I was sad to see all the old offices, once filled with passionate presenters, journalists, producers, directors, graphic designers, editors and girls in miniskirts, now filled with filing cabinets, cardboard boxes and banks of screens spewing out low-grade soaps from Australia.

But my next adventure had begun when, in 1971, I was headhunted by Mary Kenny for a brand, spanking new 'women's page' in *The Irish Press*.

THE IRISH PRESS

Now that she is identified with conservatism and Catholic journalism, it's hard to believe that Mary Kenny was the best thing that happened to women's journalism in Ireland in the 1970s. But she was. She arrived over from London's *Evening Standard* with fabulous clothes, incredible chutzpah and a brilliant eye for the zeitgeist. Appointed Women's Editor of *The Irish Press* by Tim Pat Coogan, she was given a free hand. Mind you, she probably would have taken a free hand whether it had been given or not.

'Women's pages' in newspapers before the 1970s were usually sad affairs giving the best recipes for cauliflower cheese and advising 'de lay-dies' on how to crochet bonnets for babies and look 'nice' for their husbands when they came home. In Ireland they were so bad, so dreary, so out of touch that no respectable young woman, and very few respectable older women, ever read them. Not that women's pages were new. *The Guardian* had a women's page going back to 1922, advising on 'domestic economy, labour-saving, dress, household prices and the care of children', but the Women's Editors of the 1970s – Mary Kenny at *The Irish Press*, Mary Maher at *The Irish Times* and Mary McCutcheon at the *Irish Independent* – were intent on not just upsetting the old apple cart, but also dumping the apples and the cart in the ditch and creating something entirely new, including reporting on all of the exciting developments in women's liberation movements around the world, and here in Ireland.

The pages became the first pages women – and men – turned to when they opened the paper. This was where stuff was happening. Freed from the constraints of the knitting patterns of old and the male-dominated newsrooms of the day, the women's pages invited in the best writers, hosted the brightest opinion pieces.

Mary, now a grandmother living in Kent, was a fire-cracker. No subject was taboo. In fact, the more taboo the better: wallop that wasps' nest and see what flies out. She wore outrageous clothes (her green satin hot pants have definitely gone down in history), smoked a long-stem pipe, wore hats with gigantic feathers, and pushed at every visible boundary she could find. In Ireland, just beginning to emerge from decades of Catholic and State-imposed puritanism, boundaries were everywhere. Mary stood out – a dazzlingly fearless, beautifully coloured butterfly in a dreary grey world.

Expelled from her convent boarding school at sixteen, denounced by the mother superior as 'the bad apple which rots the whole barrel' and 'the root of all evil' (Jaysus, steady on there mother superior, you're talking about a sixteen-year-old kid), Mary put her side of the story in a wonderful early piece she did for June Levine, then editing the *Irish Woman's Journal*:

They [the nuns] teach you humbleness when what you need is

confidence; passive resignation when what you need is the ability to fight and lobby for your rights; 'ladylike' attitudes when you need fundamental womanly courage and realism; conservative acceptance of all orthodox intellectual views when you need boldness of mind and intellectual muscle. And an attitude to sex, which, the world over, is recognised as turning girls either into nymphomaniacs or frigid neurotics. Maybe I'm too hard on them. After all, by expelling me, they did save me from this awful end – they admitted they hadn't tamed me.[1]

Right *on*, Sister.

She was such fun to work for, and no matter how ferocious the partying had been the night before, Mary always turned up on time, perfectly turned out and all ready to have another brilliant page ready that evening for the typesetters to 'put to bed'. She expected a similar discipline from her staff.

She had control over 'her' page; even our editor, Tim Pat Coogan, often didn't see the content until the print version appeared next morning. Poor Tim Pat. He thought he'd coaxed a bright and clever girl onto his team to bring *The Irish Press* – founded and still then owned by the deeply conservative and religious de Valera family, and traditionally a mouthpiece for Fianna Fáil – into the modern era. In truth, he'd found himself an Exocet missile.

---

1   Stopper, Anne, *Monday at Gaj's: The Story of the Irish Women's Liberation Movement* (Liffey Press, Dublin, 2006), p. 92.

THE WOMEN'S MOVEMENT

When it seemed we were doomed to stay conservative and Catholic and repressed and anti-women for evermore, where a woman's place was in the home mothering and scrubbing for evermore, some wonderful things started happening in Ireland in the early 1970s – principally the Women's Movement.

The IWLM, or the Irish Women's Liberation Movement, was a tiny group of writers, journalists, political activists, doctors, solicitors, a senator and a printer. We lasted barely nine months, but through direct action, political activism, marching, talking, shouting, more marching, as well as through journalism, sheer brass necks, determination and chutzpah, we blasted away centuries of smug patriarchy, challenged the old order and, crucially, made a space into which fledgling organisations for women could emerge.

Hurray!

I was part of that tiny band. In our short life we were denounced by politicians, by bishops, by priests, by men and by women, but by the time we'd finished, every woman in Ireland had heard our clarion call. The cat, and her kittens, were out of the bag.

When the Women's Movement got going, the forces of gombeenism and Catholicism were still riding brazenly high. It seemed impossible that our tiny little band of 'sisters', meeting every Monday night in an upstairs room in a tiny Dublin restaurant, could possibly make a dent in their armour. But we did. And the impact reached out into every home in Ireland. As Phyllis Chesler, bestselling author of *Women and Madness*, said in a 2018 Netflix documentary, *Feminists, What Were They Thinking?*, 'everything we did made the news'. The more we were denounced from the pulpits at Sunday mass, the more the politicians jeered, the more women tuned in. And turned on: why should men, particularly celibate men in frocks, control everything? Why?

Quite suddenly, everything was up for questioning. And we were off.

The 1970s was a fantastically political time. Throughout the big cities in America and Europe political unrest was everywhere, even in little old Dublin. Everyone was out marching – against the war in Vietnam, against bad housing (yup, we were being bastards to each other over housing then as well), against apartheid in South Africa, for justice in Northern Ireland, for civil rights all around the world.

News of the phenomenally successful Women's Movements in the US had been filtering across the Atlantic for some time when Máirín de Burca, the fire-starter of the Women's Movement here, and a fearsomely dedicated socialist activist, was visited by two American feminists in The Workers' Party headquarters at Gardiner Street. Her concerns about how women's rights should and could be addressed in Ireland suddenly found focus. Ireland was still a Third World country when it came to women, felt Máirín. Now she was going to try to do something about it.

No armchair activist, Máirín was involved in all of the major protest movements of the day. She'd been arrested many times and jailed for three months for smearing cow's blood on the US embassy in disgust at what was happening in Vietnam, taking the American flag down and burning it.

Máirín had left school at fourteen and was politically active at sixteen. By her mid-thirties her CV included fighting for civil rights or 'rights for black people', fighting against the Vietnam War, arguing ceaselessly against the ever-escalating war in Northern Ireland, and leaving her job to become a full-time activist, running The Workers' Party's offices and founding the Dublin Housing Action Committee.

As Margaret Gaj, owner of the eponymous Gaj's restaurant, said, Máirín was always 'one of the cleverest and most committed women' in the IWLM.

It was Máirín who made the first phone call to Mrs Gaj suggesting a women's movement, reasoning that equal rights must be fought for for all human beings. As she said, 'You couldn't discriminate. You couldn't demonstrate for Black or Native American rights without demonstrating for women.'[1]

---

1   Stopper (2006), p. 30.

Just like the American sisters who'd fought alongside men in the Civil Rights Movement, and through that had come to an awareness of their own lack of rights, Máirín said:

> the same hit us in Ireland, only slightly later because we got everything later. We had to read about it in the papers first and digest it and sort of say, 'Oh yes! This happens here too, only worse!'[2]

To test out the waters for founding a women's movement here, Máirín rang her friend, the American-born Women's Editor of *The Irish Times*, Mary Maher. Luminously beautiful and seriously clever, Mary had just returned from a visit home to Chicago and had brought with her the 'sacred texts' – the books that were changing everything: Betty Friedan's *The Feminine Mystique* and Simone de Beauvoir's *The Second Sex*. Before you could say Mary Wollstonecraft, Máirín and Mary were meeting up in Bewley's famous café on Grafton Street along with Mrs Gaj, activist Dr Moira Woods and socialist Máirín Johnston.

The five Marys/Máiríní/Moiras/Margarets.

The Women's Movement in Ireland was born.

There was a second meeting in Mary Maher's house with Máirín, Mrs Gaj and Mary, joined by Nell McCafferty,

---

2   *Ibid.*, p. 31.

Mary Anderson, Marie McMahon and me. Then a third in Mary Kenny's flat where it was settled that Mrs Gaj's restaurant in the heart of the city would be the Women's Movement's home.

First a word about Gaj's.

Margaret Gaj, always 'Mrs' Gaj, came from a Scots background, had married a Polish man (hence the name) and was a political activist to her core. Her restaurant, Gaj's, on the upper floor of an old Georgian house in Dublin, about ten minutes' walk from the Shelbourne Hotel, welcomed everyone from sex workers to aristocrats to communists to those who just wandered in off the street. Regardless of their background, Mrs Gaj sat them down to delicious plates of hot food for five shillings and sixpence. Long before hipster cafés were even dreamt of, all the tables in Gaj's were vintage 'upcycled', a nosegay of fresh flowers on each one, with Mrs Gaj on duty behind her counter just inside the door, smiling, astute, aware, overseeing a daily political, culinary and artistic 'happening'.

So there we were: Máirín de Burca, socialist and activist; Mrs Gaj, socialist, activist and restaurant owner; Mary Maher, Women's Editor of *The Irish Times*; Mary Kenny, Women's Editor of *The Irish Press*; Nell McCafferty, working-class dynamo fresh from the barricades in Derry and newly appointed star journalist with *The Irish Times*; Mary Anderson, writer and journalist, also with *The Irish Times*; Dr Moira Woods, GP, socialist and activist; June Levine, writer, journalist and, thrillingly in those days, a glamorous Jewish divorcee; Máirín Johnston, activist and socialist; Marie McMahon, socialist, activist and Ireland's youngest and only female printer; Nuala Fennell, middle-class housewife who went on to become a government minister; Mary Sheerin, secretary, journalist, writer and latterly senior press officer in the Irish government; and moi. Of course there were many, many more, including Eimer Philbin Bowman, Elgy Gillespie, Fionnuala O'Connor and Isabel Conway.

Following in the footsteps of our American sisters, we set out to be fiercely egalitarian – no one was in charge, everyone had the right to speak, and 'consciousness raising', coupled with street activism, was to be our *modus operandi*.

Two tasks were deemed in need of our urgent attention: first, to campaign for the legalisation of contraception; second, to put together a booklet outlining the dire state of women's rights in Ireland at the time.

They really were dire.

CHAINS OR CHANGE

Chains or Change, our famous pamphlet, archived in the National Library next to the Communist Manifesto, I kid you not, its yellowed Gestetnered pages showing their age, now looks like something from aeons back with its smudgy type, soft paper and rudimentary graphics. But its contents – detailing women's inequality in law, in education, in work, in marriage – are the actual Dark Ages writ large.

It was the first time anyone had even bothered to examine how women were faring in 1970s Irlanda. As American Fulbright student Anne Stopper wrote in her book, *Monday at Gaj's*: 'It [*Chains or Change*] marked the first time anyone had compiled for publication a comprehensive list of the injustices the Church, State and social code perpetuated against women.'[1]

Máirín de Burca, Mary Maher and Mary Kenny did most of the research, while Marie McMahon did the type-setting, before it was run off by June Levine and Mary Earls. Marie McMahon remembers sitting in tears after reading it, raging at the injustice of it all. Everyone in the group was shocked at how massive the discriminations against women were when they were all put together.

---

1   Stopper (2006), p. 69.

It did not make a pretty picture.

Not that prettiness was high on the agenda. For the cover page Mary Kenny wanted Liberté leading the people, breast bared Amazonian-style, as she hurrahs the people on to victory, but that was deemed too risqué. It seems funny now, but an image of the pope's hands, looking like an old woman's hands, his rosary beads redrawn as chains, was used instead.

To be honest, *Chains or Change* is not the most accessible of documents. It's strange, particularly given that so many of us were journalists, how indigestible much of the information so painfully gathered (pre-Internet days) feels. The only section with a bit of pizazz to it was Mary Maher's final chapter, 'Five Good Reasons Why it is Better to Live in Sin'. Not that it mattered. *Chains or Change* caused a sensation. It sold out as fast as we could reproduce it.

Our aims/demands as a movement were straightforward enough: fight for (i) equal pay; (ii) an end to the marriage bar for working women (the marriage bar literally meant once a woman married she had to leave her job); (iii) equal rights in law; (iv) justice for widows, 'deserted wives' and 'unmarried mothers'; (v) equal education opportunities; (vi) contraception as a human right and; (vii) one family, one house. This final clause was much fought over but adamantly advocated for by Máirín de Burca, who believed 'liberation' wouldn't be much good to women living in crap, overcrowded housing, as so many were at the time given the endemic overcrowding in housing.

We didn't include rape. We didn't include rape within marriage. We didn't include 'wife battering'. We didn't include child molestation and abuse. We didn't include incest. We didn't include rights for lesbians. We didn't include abortion.

All of these issues were huge, of course, but the brilliance of the patriarchy, as American feminist Kate Millett wrote in *Sexual Politics*, is that women internalised 'women's issues' as personal failings. If you were raped, battered, abused, deserted, it was (obviously) your fault, as a woman. You were wearing the wrong clothes, you were arguing back, you were a nag, you weren't giving him what he wanted, you were hysterical.

Besides, the assessment was that our little ship was so tiny and so fragile, and the patriarchy out there so entrenched and so vicious, that we had to start with baby steps – equal pay, equal rights, equal education, decent housing, contraception; bringing out or even discussing issues such as incest or abortion was considered too incendiary. If we went too far too fast we might alienate more women (and men) than we convinced and be closed down before we got going.

Despite our caution, the reaction from the patriarchy was still often vicious. On a march to the Dáil petitioning for the legalisation of contraception, a march that included mothers with babies and toddlers in pushchairs, with Mary Kenny leading a rousing rendition of 'We Shall Not Conceive' to the tune of 'We Shall Overcome', a red-faced bully emerged from inside the senate chamber shouting, 'Ye should all be fucked on your hands and knees like animals because that's all ye are.'

Still, while we were singing 'We Shall Not Conceive' and being cursed out of it by the august senator, three of our 'Libbers' had dodged security, climbed through an open toilet window on the ground floor, much to the surprise of the occupant, and managed to get themselves accredited and into the Seanad chamber, where Mary Robinson was on her feet, trying to get her contraception bill through.

At mass the following Sunday a certain Bishop Casey solemnly pronounced the most dangerous place to be in the world was in a mother's womb.

Oh yes, cautious and all as we usually were in the IWLM, we were poking the patriarchy as hard as we dared and it didn't like it one bit.

In 1970 advertising or selling contraceptive devices in Ireland was punishable with penal servitude. Penal servitude! Archbishop McQuaid, as powerful as any Medici potentate, sweeping through the poorest parts of Dublin in purple silks, purple hat, a huge shining black car, his august presence demanding you bowed, knelt on one knee and kissed his massive ring, had 'spies' everywhere. His power trickled down to every parish in the country, where each ordinary parish priest knew everyone's sins, everyone's failings (through the confessional), and advised and manipulated accordingly. He was simultaneously instrumental in facilitating and encouraging the 'black market' exporting of 'illegitimate' babies to America post-Second World War.[2]

The power of the Church held as long as women were not in control of whether or not they had babies. Once we in the Women's Movement began demanding contraception as a right for women, this struck at the very heart of things: if women gained control over whether or not they allowed a pregnancy to begin, they could no longer be controlled by men, particularly by the men of the Church.

Under Catholicism, everything to do with sex had become taboo, forbidden, dirty, secretive, laden with a cargo of guilt. Everything to do with sex going 'wrong', i.e. sex that produced an 'illegitimate' baby, provoked a frenzy of blame, shame, retribution.

Sex is allowable only within marriage! bellowed the Church. Sex is for the purpose of making babies, for making little Catholics! Preventing or interfering, in any way, with God's great plan every time Mammy and Daddy get it on is WRONG, EVIL and PERVERTED.

'Fuck the patriarchy!' sez we. And, 'Fuck the Church!' And give us all effective contraception while you're at it.

A – The Legal Inequities and How They Betray the Constitution

We cracked off *Chains or Change* by looking at the legal status of women in 1970s Ireland. And we didn't mince our words:

---

2   Milotte, Mike, *Banished Babies: The Secret History of Ireland's Baby Export Business* (New Island, Dublin, 2012), p. 2.

Although there has been some piecemeal reform in the legal status of married women in this country, it can still be said that upon marriage a woman in Ireland enters into a state of civil death.[3]

'Civil death' – it was horribly true.

On marrying, a woman literally became her husband's 'chattel', or 'an item of tangible, movable, personal property such as livestock, an automobile'.

- He, her husband, was the legal guardian of their children and had the sole right to decide their education, domicile and religion. Her domicile was defined as his. Even if he was living in Singapore and she in Ireland, legally her domicile was Singapore.

- He could desert her, and their children, for as long as he wished, then return and resume all marital and parental rights. She lost all of her rights – including to her children, and to her home – if she left him.

- He could divorce her in England, take the children and sell the family home, all without her knowledge or her say-so.

---

3   *Chains or Change* (Irish Women's Liberation Movement, Dublin, 1971), p. 2.

- He could have the children on his passport and take them abroad. She couldn't.

- He had total control over all money, including hers, including the Children's Allowance, including bank accounts, credit union loans, hire purchase agreements and savings.

Of course not all the men in Ireland in the 1970s were raping their wives, beating them, cheating on them, divorcing them, taking their children, selling the family home from under them and taking their money, but legally they could. The scaffolding was there within the legal system; it massively favoured the male half of the human race. We believed that only by exposing the scaffolding would real change come.

Liberation was not about becoming pseudo men, climbing into suits and joining the patriarchy; it was about dismantling the patriarchy, transforming society so that women and men would be free and equal.

B – *Chains or Change* and Work

It would be hard for the talented, confident young women of today – with their third-level education, careers and world travel under their belts – to imagine what it was like for Irish women in 1970. For starters, nobody had a 'career'; most young women had a 'job'. You stuck at the job until you had a man and a ring on your finger, then you quit. Once married, you had to quit. The infamous 'marriage bar' kicked in and back you went to your kitchen. The 'marriage bar' was mandatory in government departments and banks, and was largely employed throughout other sectors, though it was not mandatory there.

Here's what we found in *Chains or Change*:

- Irish women in 1970 were (that awful phrase) 'cheap labour'.

- Irish women occupied the lowest-grade, least-organised, lowest-status, lowest-skilled end of the labour market.

- Irish women made up a third of the workforce and only two-fifths of them were in trade unions. Women were entirely excluded from, for instance, the print unions.

- Irish women earned 54 per cent of what men earned.

- Irish women occupied only 6 per cent of administrative, executive and managerial roles.

- Irish women made up only 12 per cent of the mid professions – teachers, nurses.

- Irish women made up only 1 per cent of the higher professions – doctors, lawyers.

- All domestic servants were women. All typists were women.

- Of all the women at work, 81 per cent were single. This was largely thanks to the infamous, aforementioned 'marriage bar'.

- Of 280 trade union officials, seven were women.

C – *Chains or Change* and Education, Education, Education

In 1966, in the days when politicians actually did things for the benefit of people, as opposed to dumping €64 billion worth of failed bankers' and developers' debts on their heads and imposing 'austerity', a Fianna Fáil minister for education, Donogh O'Malley, proposed a wonderful and brilliant thing: free secondary education for all. Even more brilliantly, he announced it before a cabinet meeting had even discussed the measure, never mind ratified it, leaving no room for ifs, buts or maybes.

The effect was invaluable. In a few short generations the young people of Ireland leapt forward a century as thousands of Irish parents grabbed the opportunity to help their kids up their game; also, perhaps unwittingly, freeing them from the shackles of post-colonial conservatism and Catholicism.

It's easy to sneer now at how girls used to be educated in Ireland, how ridiculously crippling and sexist the notions pushed onto them were, but the prevailing reality for most women at that time was: the men had the money; therefore, in order to get at money you had to 'get a man'. Getting a man was deemed far more important than getting an education, going on to university or thinking of a career.

Mary Kenny told June Levine in *Sisters*, 'out of eighteen girls in my sister's class of 1956, sixteen became secretaries'. Sixteen out of eighteen – and these were the elite![4]

---

4   Levine, June, *Sisters: The Personal Story of an Irish Feminist* (Attic

In *Chains or Change* we found that 'any outside job [for women] is either a stopgap between school, marriage and babies, or a financial necessity for a widow, single woman or deserted wife'. And, 'the early education of the vast majority of girls ensures that they never think of breaking into a "male" enclave, but regard their "real" career as that of a wife and mother'.[5]

When it came to education I was in the 'privileged' bracket, educated by the Sacred Heart nuns first at a day school and later at a boarding school. The nuns weren't all bad, but the fact that the entire country, apart from a tiny cohort of non-Catholics, was being educated by religious celibates was crazy. When it came to 'sexual education' things with the nuns got pretty weird – 'the minute the key goes in the ignition the mortal sin begins'; 'your body is the temple of the Holy Ghost and nothing must sully it'; 'French kissing is a mortal sin for which you will go to hell for all eternity'; 'Self-love is no love', etc., etc.

During one three-day religious retreat, everyone in the school – junior girls, senior girls, day girls, nuns, cleaners, sisters – all had to be silent, morning, meal times, evenings, nights. We older girls crammed into the little chapel night after night to hear the visiting priest's lecture. Apart from the grey-haired priest who usually said mass and the thinly

---

Press, Dublin, 2009), p. 114.

5   *Chains or Change* (1971), p. 10.

thatched gardener who tended the veg garden, this priest was the only 'man' we would see for weeks on end. To add sauce to the fiery mix of days of silence, incense, prayers, hymns and raging teenage hormones, this particular priest was an American.

Jesus, the excitement.

Very little of what he said made sense, but on the third night he dropped his bombshell: unauthorised sex, he pronounced from the altar – that is, sex of ANY kind outside marriage – would inevitably result in syphilis or VD. Graphic descriptions of the horrors of venereal disease followed. What? We didn't even know what sex was – other than this powder keg about to blow – and now we were being told it would lead us straight to hell and VENEREAL DISEASE.

That evening our comprehensive ignorance on all matters sexual was backlit with violent, not-easily-forgotten images of bodies rotting from the inside out.

The 'ideal' of womanhood on offer was: humble, pious, self-sacrificing, 'natural-born' mothers. An ideal that, as Geraldine Meany wrote in 1993 in her *Sex and Nation*, led to self-hatred and hatred of their own sex for some women, who still, up to today:

> seek to perpetuate the idealised virgin/mother figure of woman so that they can *be* that figure. The attractions of the traditional feminine role, particularly as the Catholic church defines it, are grounded in a deep distrust and loathing of

femininity, however, and those women who identify with it are also expressing a form of self-hatred, a revulsion against themselves as women. They are unable to accept themselves as thinking, choosing, sexual, intellectual and complex ordinary mortals and instead cling to a fantasy of women as simple handmaids of the lord.[6]

Oh yes indeedy, simple handmaids to the Lord and, conveniently, scrubbers, cooks, toilet cleaners, baby makers and childminders for the men.

We were like battery hens, schooled from the year dot into becoming 'mammies', convinced that by staying inside the cages so helpfully and carefully constructed by Church and State, we were free.

Everything within the education system militated against our becoming thinking, independent creatures. Little girls were encouraged to play with dolls and cookery sets ('just like mammies'); little boys got guns, chemistry sets and bicycles.

Little girls were taught how to clean, how to make beds, how to cook; little boys were taught how to plonk their asses on a seat and wait for their sisters and mammies to serve them.

Little girls did 'domestic science' – sewing, cooking. Little boys did chemistry, biology, carpentry.

Little girls could NOT do maths. It was a well-known

---

6   Meaney, Geraldine, *Sex and Nation: Women in Irish Culture and Politics* (Attic Press, University of Virginia, 1991), p. 232.

and scientifically proven FACT that their female constitutions prohibited them from understanding numbers.

In case we forget, this crappy propaganda worked a treat: in 1968 only 161 girls took maths at Leaving Certificate level; 2,000 boys did.

In 1963, of those pupils who achieved an honours Leaving Certificate, 43 per cent of boys went on to university and only 19 per cent of girls.

In 1969 we found, at University College Dublin, 'only four girls [were] doing agriculture, fifteen doing dentistry and sixteen veterinary medicine – out of a total of 3,494 female students'.

As the appointments officer at the university said, 'Too many talented girls restrict themselves: they think, "I'm 21 and have a degree, I'll work for a couple of years, then get married and stop work."'[7]

Girls and women were systematically blocked when it came to thinking of a 'career', i.e. something satisfying that would make them real money. Maths was the biggest block. Since right through their education girls were discouraged from taking maths, and since many of the most lucrative professions demanded a higher maths qualification – accountancy, engineering, science, veterinary medicine – most girls were stopped before they'd got started.

Astonishingly, we found that only 10 per cent of girls'

7   *Chains or Change* (1971), p. 13.

schools at the time even offered the honours-level maths curriculum. Ten per cent!

Strangely, even though the data we dug up was so incontrovertible – that girls were still being educated to be 'mammies, carers, handmaidens to the Lord', etc. – we 'liberated', educated careerists sounded a rather tentative note on the women and maths issue:

> There is a long tradition in education of conditioning women into believing that they are not 'naturally' good at Maths subjects. The only real evidence is purely circumstantial and no one knows for sure whether the observed low standard in women's general aptitude for spatial concepts is innate or the product of many generations of such deep psychological conditioning.[8]

Of course it was due to generations of deep psychological conditioning! But even we weren't 100 per cent sure if we ladies could be so bold as to use a mathematical term here. Sarcasm aside, it indicates how deep the conditioning was, even among us sisters.

In 1972 I wrote a novel: *Fathers Come First*. Rereading it for republication in 2015, I found my twenty-something heroine Lizzie saying:

> I never thought money important. Money was a huge safe that

---

8   *Chains or Change* (1971), pp. 11–12.

men had the key to and you just had to get a man and then you got the money. Some men got a little, some a lot, you just had to choose the right man. First there were fathers, and then there were boyfriends, and then there were lovers, and then you thought, well, then there'll be husbands. Certainly money wasn't important.[9]

Sure I was channelling my teenage self, but how thoroughly, I thought, she had swallowed the propaganda. How heedlessly she had thrown herself onto the mercy of men. How little she thought of her 'well-educated' self.

D – *Chains or Change* and Jobs and Marriage

Our fourth section of *Chains or Change* examined the barriers against women fully entering the workforce. Jesus, what am I saying? For most women, entering the workforce – other than as a skivvy, telephonist or a typist on shit wages – was a brutal obstacle course.

These are some of the careers we found were entirely closed to women: airline pilots, bus drivers, police inspectors, bank managers, newspaper editors, newspaper compositors, criminal lawyers and engineers. Others that ranged from almost impossible to very restricted included: judges, surgeons, technicians, accountants and higher civil servants.

---

9   Sweetman, Rosita, *Fathers Come First* (Lilliput Press, Dublin, 2015), p. 10.

Those few women who did get through the obstacle course were haunted by the delightful slur – hurled by both men and other women – that they would 'lose their femininity'. Hah! Scrubbing toilets all day for a pittance was grand but getting near the top of the tree, earning a decent salary, endangered your 'womanliness'. And just in case we ladies got too demanding, as soon as we got married the marriage bar kicked in, only ending in 1957 for primary teachers, in 1973 for civil servants and not until 1977 for all, when the Employment Equality Act prohibited discrimination on the grounds of gender or marital status in all areas of employment.

You've got to hand it to the patriarchs: they thought of everything.

We found 'a fear inherent in women that men dislike successful career women' and that 'there exists among men a reluctance to work for women', concluding meekly that 'this may be a product of social conditioning'.[10]

I love the 'may be'.

E – *Chains or Change* and Women in Distress

If you thought women typists, telephonists and the married were having a hard time under the Irish patriarchy, unbelievably thin gruel was being handed out to the ladies who fell outside of the patriarchy's net. We covered them under one of the longest sections in the pamphlet, 'Women

---

10   *Chains or Change* (1971), p. 15.

in Distress', broken down into 'widow', 'deserted wife', 'unmarried mother' and 'the single woman'. The designations alone still give me the shivers.

In brief, the trajectory of deprivation from widow to deserted wife to unmarried mother was steeply downwards, with especially vicious opprobrium – from women as well as men – for the unmarried mother.

Interestingly, widows in Ireland were one of the first groups of women who banded together. June Levine saw them, and the Irish Housewives Association, as being ahead of their time in their recognition of the relationship between the personal and the political.[11]

Times for widows were extremely hard. Once a woman had lost the protection of a man, she often found herself, along with her family, virtually penniless, not to mention losing her place and voice in society. As journalist Gráinne Farren wrote: 'Totally dependent on their husbands, married women were stuck for life, as divorce was forbidden. Single mothers, widows and deserted wives faced dire poverty.'[12]

The widow's pension was then £5 a week, with 50p extra for every dependent child; some nasty anomalies were thrown in for working widows. Of the 126,000 widows in Ireland at the time, 28,000 were working, usually out of desperation and despite the losses full-time working imposed on them

---

11   Stopper (2006), pp. 127–30.
12   *Irish Independent*, 21 May 2006.

and their families, like half-rate benefits for widows who fell sick; automatic loss of non-contributory pension; four times the rent of her male equivalent in corporation housing. Not what you might call a win-win situation.

When it came to 'the deserted wife', things were even more dire.

Divorce was taboo in Ireland up until 1996. Enshrined in the Irish Constitution in 1937, next to pregnancy outside marriage, divorce was the big bogeyman. Legalising divorce was clearly going to make all happily married couples look at each other the next morning over the cornflakes and scream: 'I HATE YOU! I AM DIVORCING YOU IMMEDIATELY!'

As with its attitude to sex education – if you don't tell them about it, they won't do it – the Church was the main player in the brainwashing: all the men will leave – in the morning! All marriages will crash – this afternoon! All women and children will be left dying and crying on the streets – by tomorrow night!

The prohibition on divorce led to Ireland's 'deserted wives' phenomenon, whereby a man fed up with his matri-monial arrangements headed off to England or America, or wherever, and simply 'disappeared', leaving wife and children with no legal protection whatsoever.

Desertion of wives and children was rife. The 1966 census showed 11,300 men were 'absent from home'. In the first six months of 1969 alone, we discovered, 600 husbands had abandoned their wives and families. Gone AWOL. And since Irish courts wouldn't recognise English divorce laws, English courts wouldn't recognise Irish court orders. The men were never tracked down. The women and the kiddies were the outright losers.

It wasn't until 1970 that a social welfare bill was brought in recognising 'deserted wives' as a group and awarding them and their children a pittance.

When we looked at the situation of 'unmarried mothers' in *Chains or Change*, we ourselves were in many ways a bit naïve.

By 1970 locking up vulnerable pregnant women, often for life, was as far as the Irish State had got in terms of 'dealing' with the issue of pregnancy outside marriage. Pregnancy outside marriage still being entirely 'the fault' of women. Girls 'fell'. Boys 'sowed their wild oats'. Even in 1970 a woman who became pregnant 'outside marriage' was on her own. In 1969 we found out that a handful, or 250 women, mostly middle class, were able to go to Britain for an abortion. The less well off were turfed out of the family, and into a Mother and Baby, home. A few went to London 'for a holiday' and came back sans baby – baby had been sent off for adoption. It's safe to say that many parents would have preferred for their child to take drugs rather than have a baby. You could hide drugs, but you couldn't hide a baby.

Many of the girls who did become pregnant, who managed to avoid being incarcerated in a Mother and Baby Home, were so terrified, that the first time they visited a doctor or hospital was when they went into labour. For many who did finally get to a hospital to give birth, the Catholic Rescue Society would be there, waiting to take baby away for adoption, no matter how loudly mum screamed and cried.

We did our best with the knowledge we had then, but I think if we were writing now about 'the unmarried mother' in traditional, patriarchal Ireland, our pens would drip with so much rage at what was done to these girls and women and their babies that they would burn the paper they were writing on.

Un-fucking-married indeed.

Shamefully, we perpetrated our own bit of patronising claptrap vis-à-vis unmarried mothers, writing: 'We need a central organisation which will help and rehabilitate the unmarried mother.'

Rehabilitate? These days that sounds scarily akin to the Mother and Baby Homes philosophy, in which 'the fallen' ones were to be 'rehabilitated' by slaving in laundries or scrubbing floors for the rest of their lives. As Maura Richards wrote in her 1998 memoir, *Single Issue*:

> Even within the IWLM others were talking on our behalf and patronisingly suggesting we needed 'rehabilitation' not liberation. The idea of unmarried mothers acting for themselves had not entered their minds.[13]

---

13   Richards, Maura, *Single Issue* (Poolbeg, Dublin, 1998), p. 49.

As for Mother and Baby Homes, shamefully, we middle-class girls only had an inkling of what these places were like. It would be another twenty years before the silence and secrecy surrounding these 'homes' would start to lift, when Mary Raftery began her exposé of systemic sexual, emotional and physical abuse in religious-led, State-financed, industrial schools and reformatories. This was followed by a slow trickle of information emerging around the Mother and Baby Homes.

F – *Chains or Change* and Why It's Better to Live in Sin

In our final section, entitled 'Five Good Reasons Why it is Better to Live in Sin', we gave the 'single woman' five good reasons for partnering up without tying the knot:

(i)   you get to keep your job

(ii)   your income tax doesn't go up

(iii) you maintain your separate business identity

(iv) you retain your right to at least negotiate how things go down in the home, and

(v)   you remain your own 'property' and do not become the chattel of a man.

Yes, you couldn't get a mortgage or credit of any kind, even hire purchase, without a male guarantor, but you were definitely better off, legally and financially, than your married sisters.

G – *Chains or Change* and Incidental Facts

In the section named 'Incidental Facts', we placed the contraception issue, then the hottest topic for women here, under *Incidental Fact number one*: 'Artificial birth control' is illegal in Ireland, as is the dissemination of any or all information about birth control,' we wrote. 'By a nice trick of public hypocrisy,' we went on, 'the contraceptive pill is permitted since it is imported into Ireland merely as a "cycle regulator"…To employ any other device is to break the law.'[14]

Since 1935 the import and sale of all contraceptive devices was banned, but not their use. Those with money could get them, but buying them in a chemist was impossible. Veteran activist and founding member of the Irish Family Planning Association Frank Crummey was once stopped by gardaí coming back from the North with 40,000 condoms bought legally from the London Rubber Company in Portadown. He managed to blag his way through on the grounds that they were for his personal use. Wink wink, nudge nudge. And since many Irish GPs were aware of the desperation of parents to control their family size, by the 1970s 25,000 Irish women were on the pill legally, prescribed as a 'cycle regulator'; in essence, women who had the information, the money and a fair-minded doctor could get themselves the pill. However, for women living outside Dublin, for working-class women, for women who didn't have a sympathetic doctor, getting hold of

---

14   *Chains or Change* (1971), p. 25.

contraceptives was difficult to impossible.

Máirín Johnston remembers discreet advertisements in English magazines for women offering 'rubber goods under plain cover' and a PO Box number. The 'rubber goods' being condoms 'you could mend a bicycle tyre with'.

Incidental Fact number two looked at divorce. Ireland was among the last seven [western] countries in the world to have no divorce. Clearly this backfired horribly on women and children as, when husbands deserted them, the women and children left behind had no legal recourse here or in England.

Incidental Fact number three looked at what we called 'baby minding'. We found it was completely unregulated, 'hazardous and unprotected by the law', with no State- or local authority-run nursery schools or crèches. And it was also cripplingly expensive, with playground facilities 'remarkably bad'.

Incidental Fact number four looked at retraining facilities for mature women to come back to the workforce. There weren't any! Or what was there was pitiful to non-existent. Stacking shelves in supermarkets was the best many mature women coming back to work could expect.

Our final *Incidental Fact* was a truly bizarre reminder of the scorn in which the Catholic Church held women. Under Catholic doctrine, women were not allowed to read the 'Epistle' in church. We were deemed too 'impure'. Women were not allowed inside the altar rails of a Catholic church except as skivvies or, briefly, as brides.

And we didn't even mention 'churching', a practice dropped after the Second Vatican Council in 1967 whereby mothers were brought into the church to be blessed after the 'taint' of childbirth.

H – *Chains or Change* and Women and Taxation

When it came to our penultimate chapter, 'Women and Taxation', things remained stark. As soon as a woman married her income became assessed along with her husband's, and he received all of the tax allowances. She paid approximately a third of her income in tax, whereas he paid a fifth. Working widows were refused a married person's allowance despite having to run a home and bring up children just like their male married counterparts.

Oh yes, the patriarchs had thought of everything.

Now a historic document, what *Chains or Change* uncovered – the systematic favouring of males over females in marriage, in family, in law, in education, in finance, in tax, in social mores – was irrefutable. That this was the first time in Ireland that the patriarchy's structure had been exposed and pinned, quivering, into a thirty-one-page black-and-white booklet was remarkable in itself.

Next we needed to bring our findings to a national audience.

THE LATE LATE SHOW

It was decided, or rather Mary Kenny, the out-and-out flamboyant butterfly of the movement and the media darling of the day, decided, that launching *Chains or Change* on *The Late Late Show* would be a brilliant idea. She saw it as a peerless way for us to get information about the IWLM, plus everything we'd uncovered in *Chains or Change*, out to the general public.

Mary had made contact, by chance, with Pan Collins, who was herself a bit of a media legend, having the ear of one of the powerbrokers of the day, Gay Byrne, the big jolly uncle to the nation, and presenter of *The Late Late Show*. Supposedly a light-entertainment, late-night Saturday show, in fact *The Late Late* was often an arena par excellence where the social and political issues of the day could be aired and fought over. It was where the country came to meet itself.

Mary, with her genius for publicity, realised getting *The Late Late* would rush us to the forefront of public debate. But first, she would invite Pan Collins to come along to Gaj's and meet 'the sisters', having a pretty good idea that Pan would fall for us hook, line and sinker.

When Mary announced her plan at the Monday evening meeting in Gaj's, people went crazy. Who the hell was Mary Kenny to decide that we should go on *The Late Late* with herself, no doubt about it, centre stage? Who said going public was a good idea anyway? How were we to know Gay wouldn't turn the whole thing into a circus, make eejits of us?

Mary, using her best convent-girl manners, soothed feathers so effectively that by the end of the (uproarious) evening she had her way: Pan Collins was to be invited to an evening of 'Monday at Gaj's'.

June Levine, later to become a researcher on *The Late Late* herself, asked Pan many years later what she made of this gaggle of young feminists. Pan admitted she was both a bit 'disgusted' and very 'delighted'. She realised she had struck gold for her boss; that we wild, blue-jeaned ones could be relied upon to 'rant and rave, forget the camera, entertain the viewers, bring in showers of protesting letters, keep Gay Byrne happy'. Basically, we would be 'good telly'.[1]

Actually we worked very hard to make sure things stayed calm and, in truth, Mary Kenny had wangled a pretty good deal. Not only would we get *The Late Late* (6 March 1971), we would also get to decide who would be on the panel. After much discussion, we finally chose a very respectable one, including our legal eagle Senator Mary Robinson, historian Mary Cullen, television producer Lelia Doolan, and two members of the IWLM, Máirín Johnston and Nell McCafferty. Other members and supporters were scattered throughout the audience.

---

1   Levine (2009), p. 159.

All went smoothly, at first. Mary Robinson discussed the legal inequalities under which women suffered. Mary Cullen addressed problems faced by working mothers. Lelia Doolan spoke about the miseducation of girls. Máirín Johnston spoke about job discrimination, and Nell spoke about widows, deserted wives, unmarried mothers.

Suddenly, from the audience, Mary Kenny got up and said she didn't think any of our public representatives gave a damn about women's rights. It was akin to chucking a hand grenade into a bonfire. Before you could say 'political opportunity!', Garret FitzGerald, then leader of the opposition, 'left his fireside', so outraged was he at Mary's slur. He was, of course, ushered straight into the studios and onto the set.

This was television gold.

The rest of the show didn't turn out to be quite the mature, reasoned, reasonable exposition of the rights of women for which we'd hoped and drilled. Once on the panel, 'Garret the Good' had a great time telling everyone in his big booming man's voice how brilliant things were going to be for women once he got in. The studio duly exploded. There was lots and lots of screaming. We thought we'd arranged for every eventuality on *The Late Late*, but we'd never foreseen a six-foot-something upper-middle-class politician parachuting in and taking over.

Lots of good points were still made. Nell McCafferty managed to skewer Garret on his not voting against the Forcible Entry Bill (a draconian piece of legislation principally designed to arrest and criminalise families squatting in vacant properties managed by the Dublin Housing Action Committee). Marxists pointed out that capitalism oppressed both women and men. June attacked married women for being so complacent in their married bliss that they were blind to their own precarious position, as well as that of their sisters. Mary Robinson began, 'There is a Department of Justice', and was howled down by roars of derision. A representative from the Women's Progressive Association said it was up to the women to change things, that the conditioning of girls and boys began in the home so had to be changed in the home. And the whole tumultuous evening was topped off with a terrific speech by Mary Kenny, who said:

> Women won't, can't, get together until the inequities have been removed, until the social condition of women has changed and until the whole system has changed. They will stay at home passively, [where] they're safe, they're married, they don't care about other people. That's where liberation comes in and that's where we're going to start.

Rousing stuff! And if the show hadn't gone with the exquisite taste, calm exposition and perfect control we'd hoped for, and even if Garret the Good had taken over, by the next morning everyone in Ireland who wasn't living under a rock knew that modern feminism had arrived in Ireland, that the Irish

Women's Liberation Movement was her voluble mouthpiece, and *Chains or Change* her manifesto.

Huzzah!

Sadly, and rather weirdly, not a single taped copy of that famous baptism of fire exists. Not one.

Still, barely a month after *The Late Late* appearance, we called for a public meeting in the Round Room of the Mansion House, terrified we would be the only people there. However, over a thousand super-enthusiastic women turned up. Among them was Helen Heaphy, who stood up and said, to sustained thunderous applause, 'My name is Helen Heaphy and I am an unmarried mother.' It was the first time ever that the label had been publicly 'owned'.[2]

What a day! Women from all over Ireland finding and embracing each other; finding and embracing the truth of their lives. Women's Lib had truly arrived.

---

2   *Ibid.*, p. 172.

THE CONTRACEPTIVE TRAIN

The 'Contraceptive Train' was our most successful direct-action protest. It was Nell McCafferty and Mary Maher's brilliant brainchild. And it was Mary Maher's idea that the action should take place on World Media Day. It was not by chance that the return into Connolly Station was captured on film.

The idea was simple: a bunch of us women would jump on the train to Belfast – where contraceptives were legal – buy pills, come home, swallow them in front of the customs officers waiting at the station, and dare them to jail us.

We would boldly call out the law, challenge the men of the law to arrest us, show the law to be a hypocritical ass and, hopefully, usher in contraception for all.

Forty-seven women boarded the train for Belfast on 22 May 1971. Bad me, I wasn't one of them. It was my twenty-third birthday and I stayed in bed with my man, Prince Charming, who had returned to me, claiming to have missed me terribly, and who, ironically, since he was English, had plenty of contraceptives.

The sisterhood was, understandably, unimpressed. Nell still says, 'You stepped out of history, Rosita.'

Foolish me!

Still, I was there for the sisters' homecoming, which was

organised by Máirín de Burca. I remember yelling, 'Let them through! Let them through!' with the best of them.

By all accounts things had been pretty interesting on the journey. For starters, when the women poured into a Belfast chemist, they were stunned to be informed that the contraceptive pill was available on prescription only. The same went for a coil or IUD. Disaster! Undaunted, and after a quick confab, Nell suggested buying hundreds of aspirin – after all, what customs officer in Dublin would know, or dare to find out, the difference? Aspirin were duly bought, along with spermicidal jelly and Durex 'sheaths'.

Job done, the women split up and took advantage of Belfast's cheap shopping, assembling for the journey home elated and a bit scared. What kind of reception would they get when they returned? Would some of them face jail? What about their mammies? How disgusted would they be with their scarlet daughters flaunting contraceptives?

Nell McCafferty and Mary Anderson had arranged free legal aid and, just in case, a helpful list of options if a customs officer did pull us up:

- Declare nothing and risk being searched.

- Declare contraceptives and refuse to be searched.

- Declare contraceptives and refuse to hand over.

- Declare contraceptives and hand over with protest of infringement of your constitutional rights.

- Declare contraceptives and throw over barrier to sisters waiting beyond. Many people who couldn't come today will be demonstrating at Amiens Street in solidarity with our action.

- Declare contraceptives and sit down in anticipation of customs action.

- Declare internal contraceptive. Allow search from female officer only and shout 'April Fool' before entry.

In her classic book *Sisters*, June Levine describes how other women on the train were less than pleased to have their own shopping trips highlighted to the customs men. As the train got closer to Dublin, everyone started piling on newly bought gear under their normal clothes.

Máirín Johnston, five months pregnant and with her partner and fourteen-year-old son in tow, started to get really scared. Talking about it, planning it, making the huge banner in her kitchen the night before – all that had been fun. Now the reality of it was here and it was frightening. Would she be jailed? Would other sisters? Marie McMahon was terrified her mother would find out; she'd sent her sister and her sister's kids up to her mum's house to create a ruckus so that her mother would miss the six o'clock news. Marie said the most thrilling part of the journey was leaning out the window of the train as they approached Dublin's Connolly Station and hearing voices in the distance shouting, 'Let them through!' There was a huge welcome home party! In full cry! Everything was going to be okay.

In the end, everything was okay. A very white-faced Máirín Johnston was delegated to go up to the first customs officer, show him the spermicidal jelly she'd bought and refuse to hand it over. Máirín said he was more terrified than she was. 'It's spermicidal jelly. It's mine. You can't have it.' Other women swallowed aspirin in front of other officers. Everyone crammed in behind the wonderful banner, fists raised, as those of us in the welcome party bellowed support. The cameramen so conveniently there – thank you Mary Maher – captured it all: the defiant young women; the embarrassed customs officers; the handfuls of 'pills' being chucked in the air as someone shouted theatrically, 'Loose your contraceptives!'

Nobody was arrested. Nobody was even shoved around. Nobody knew it was just aspirin being thrown or swallowed. The trip had been a triumph. Hypocrisy was laid bare.

We were called harlots, man haters, lesbians, baby killers, etc., and it took another twenty-one years before contraception was finally and fully legalised for all, but yanking the issue out into the public arena, politicising it, was game-changing.

At a mass the following week, Bishop of Clonfert Thomas Ryan said from the altar: 'Not since penal times has the Catholic heritage of Ireland been subjected to so many insidious onslaughts, on the pretext of conscience, civil rights and women's liberation.'[1]

He was right. We were determined the 'Catholic heritage of Ireland' should be dismantled, particularly when it came to women.

It still took years to bring about, of course. When introducing the half-baked Family Planning Act of 1979 that gave married couples the right to contraception, Charles Haughey commended it to the Dáil as an 'Irish solution to an Irish problem'. Deputy Noël Browne rejected this claim, pointing out instead that the bill was '"riddled" with the "Catholic sectarianism of Irish republicanism"'. And we didn't want an 'Irish solution to an Irish problem'; we wanted a modern set of laws ensuring access to contraception for anybody and everybody who wanted it and needed it.[2]

On Miriam O'Callaghan's show on RTÉ Radio on 27 September 2015, marking the debut of a musical by Arthur Riordan and *Riverdance* muso Bill Whelan based around the 'Contraceptive Train', Máirín de Burca recalled being questioned all day, in a very hostile manner, by a garda sergeant and an inspector some weeks later on a completely separate matter. Somehow the conversation came round to contraception. One garda piped up 'there's always the

---

1   Bourke, Angela (ed.), *The Field Day Anthology of Irish Writing: Volume V, Irish Women's Writing and Tradition* (New York University Press, New York, 2002), pp. 200–1.

2   TheJournal.ie, 30 December 2012, https://www.thejournal.ie/read-me/contraception-in-ireland-and-haughey-723161-Dec2012/.

rhythm method', to which Máirín replied, 'that's fine if the woman's cycle is regular. Very many women's are not.'

'She's dead right, you know' was the sergeant's heartfelt reply.

Máirín felt curiously vindicated; we'd brought the issue of contraception out of the closet and into the public forum, where it could be properly discussed. Even with arresting policemen!

Arise!

THE BEGINNING OF THE END

After the triumph of the publication of *Chains or Change*, our appearance on *The Late Late Show*, the subsequent monster meeting in the Mansion House and the wildly successful 'Contraceptive Train' to Belfast, we were riding high. Sadly, though none of us knew it at the time, we were riding towards our end.

One by one, the founding members left or fell by the wayside. Mary Kenny, the rebellious, outrageous, impossible-to-control self-selected spokeswoman, left first to go work in London. It was like a great fire went out, particularly as Mary didn't just leave all of us behind but – at first gradually and then almost totally – left the ideas of feminism behind as well. As far as we were concerned she was a complete turncoat. A traitor of the highest order. We also felt that, as far as she was concerned, we were bitter, unforgiving, twisted harridans, unable to see the subtleties of life, the changes and commitments marriage and motherhood bring. When I spoke to Mary recently about it she said she *never* thought of us as 'bitter, unforgiving, twisted harridans'. The very idea! But she admitted that, yes, she had jumped ship, mainly, she said, because she had a monstrous ego and desperately wanted the *Evening Standard* job in London, even though it turned out to be awful.

Nuala Fennell, another of the founding members, left in a blaze of bitter publicity. The split was eagerly lapped up by broadsheets and red-tops alike, with Nuala saying, 'Women's lib has not only lost her virginity but has turned into a particularly nasty harlot.' She added that membership of the IWLM required one to be 'anti-American, anti-clerical, anti-government, anti-Irish Countrywomen's Association, anti-police and anti-men'. A broad-brush condemnation that painted us all as freakish, middle-class wannabe revolutionaries who didn't have a clue how to actually change things.[1]

Ouch.

Naturally, Nuala's defection and broadside caused rage and distress, but she had a driving need to be practical. Within weeks of leaving she was scrubbing toilets in a borrowed house in the city, opening the first-ever battered wives' hostel with her husband. She went on to become a feminist icon in her own right, first as a councillor, then a TD and finally a minister in government.

At Gaj's, the Monday evenings were becoming in-creasingly difficult to manage, with new members crowding in and the original sisters being accused of arrogance and elitism. It seemed unbearably sad and horrible at the time, but, looking back, maybe we had done our job as far as we could and dissolution was the logical next step. We'd shown,

---

1   Stopper (2006), p. 151.

in detail, what was wrong. Now it was time for all the other women in the country to start to put it right.

Either way, the centre was not holding. Mary Kenny was now 'utterly miserable' inside a huge *Evening Standard* newsroom in London. Máirín Johnston was having another baby. Mary Maher was bringing up two babies and holding down her job as editor of the 'women's page' in *The Irish Times*. Nuala Fennell was busy setting up organisations that helped women practically. Nell McCafferty had gone to France, then returned and joined 'Irish Women Unite'. Maura Woods withdrew to nurse her dying husband.

As Máirín Johnston said to me during the summer of 2019, 'We weren't a political party. We had different views on everything. So different women left to do what they were interested in. But we'd given all women the voice to protest.'

Was it all over? Or had we cracked open the ground sufficiently, scattered the seeds of liberation ubiquitously enough that growth would spring up in our wake, with new groups addressing the issues we had highlighted?

Luckily, it was the latter, and while those of us in the founding group took off to pastures new, or returned to pastures old, the magic lantern had been rubbed and the Women's Movement unleashed. No amount of yelling from the pulpit, at dinner parties, in the bedroom, at workplaces or on building sites was going to shove it back. It had been a somewhat chaotic birthing, but the Women's Movement – the awareness of how crappy things had been for women in Ireland for so long – was here and things would never be quite so crappy for Irish women again.

After the IWLM had limped towards its demise, other battles continued. Mary Robinson kept politely hammering away at the law. Irish Women United took up the liberation baton and staged some terrific direct-action coups. One was the invasion of the 'men only' bathing spot in Sandy-cove, incidentally (wouldn't you know) the nicest swimming hole on the Dublin coast – a pristine, deep-water sanctuary bounded by huge granite boulders where the gents, emphasising their hegemony, bathed nude, women and kiddies consigned to a filthy beach nearby. After several 'invasions' by the ladies – thrillingly by land and sea – the men backed down, put their trunks back on and agreed, albeit reluctantly, to 'share'.

Another bit of nonsense that Nell successfully challenged was the idea of women not being allowed in pubs on their own and not being allowed to buy pints. With thirty women in tow, she stood at the bar in Neary's, off Grafton Street, and ordered up thirty brandies and one pint. When the barman refused to serve the pint, the women drank up their brandies and left.

'He didn't serve. We didn't pay.'[2]

Another day the women climbed into the hallowed, all-male preserve of the Fitzwilliam Lawn Tennis Club, where

---

2   *Timeline*, 17 May 2017.

they proceeded to play 'bad sets' (i.e. deliberately slow, bad play).

On yet another occasion Nell was in the foyer of the Shelbourne Hotel when the minister for foreign affairs, and later president, Paddy Hillery arrived. Nell grabbed him by the tie and shoved him up against the wall, saying, 'Women want contraception, NOW.' Afterwards the doorman approached: the barmen had set up a brandy for her at the bar.

Yay!

One protest involved a young woman going out to the hideous Papal Cross in Phoenix Park, erected after the visit of Pope John Paul II in 1979. Across its massive concrete plinth she spray-painted Gloria Steinem's great battle cry: 'If men got pregnant, contraception and abortion would be sacraments.' The next week every JCB in the country was pressed into service, the plinth and the offending graffiti earthed up forever.

One of the things the Women's Movement achieved was bringing issues previously hidden out into the public domain. Writing in her column in *The Irish Press* in 1985, Nell McCafferty remembered:

> Child sexual abuse is not a new phenomenon. What is new is
> the public admission that it happens, and our attempts to cope
> with it. As with the revelations in the 1970s of widespread
> wife-battery and rape, and reaction to these revelations – dis-
> belief, ignorance, the first faltering attempts of underfunded

voluntary agencies to cope, the establishment of official chan-
nels, the first surfacing in court, the fumbling reaction of the
judiciary, and then the legal measures – so it is now with child
abuse.[3]

Or as Mary Leland said at a book launch in the Irish Writers
Centre in 2003:

> I also wonder now at the stories that we missed, like child
> sexual abuse. We simply had no idea but I wonder now: why?
> Where was I in the 1970s? Was it all so closed off that we
> weren't even curious?[4]

I think it was. And we weren't.

---

3   *The Irish Press*, 15 August 1985.
4   *The Irish Times*, 13 September 2003 – *Changing the Times*, launch at
     the Irish Writers Centre, 2003, https://www.irishtimes.com/news/
     women-on-the-front-line-1.375669.

LOOKING BACK

Looking back, alongside our successes in the IWLM, we left some serious gaps – most crucially, the issue of work and what happens when the babies come along. Many of us were young and childless and didn't see that particular gap yawning. We talked vaguely about 'baby minding' being expensive, crèches not being provided freely by local authorities – bless our innocence – but the politics of dividing labour and responsibility equally when the kiddies arrive, the possibility of how women could stay in the workforce without being crucified, didn't get our full attention.

It's a sad testament to male-centric capitalism, and our failure as feminists to tackle it, that liberating women from the home has meant saddling the men and women of today with mortgages so high it takes both of their salaries to meet them. And on top of that the working parents of today have to pay the equivalent of a second mortgage for childcare.

Oh yes, there is still a long, long way to go.

THE RISING WAVES OF FEMINISM

SECTION IV

FEMINISM'S FOREMOTHERS
IN AMERICA

Let's go Stateside, where the *fabulous* second-wave American sisters had been kicking seventeen kinds of crap out of the patriarchy for a good decade before we got going here. Being American they had cut straight to the chase. None of your leafleting or shilly-shallying around, militant activism was at the movement's core.

What's known as 'second-wave feminism' had its immediate roots in the Civil Rights Movement of the 1960s, with agitations and huge social unrest right across America.

Its deeper roots were in the nineteenth-century Abolition of Slavery Movement, and the birthing of Women's Suffrage. Hats off here to the two extraordinary Grimké sisters, fearless early feminists of that time who linked patriarchy and slavery: 'we [women] are much in the same situation of the slave. Man has asserted an assumed authority over us ...'

Or again:

I believe it will be found that men, in the exercise of their usurped dominion over women, have almost invariably done one of two things. They have either made slaves of the creatures whom God designed to be their companions and their coadjutors in every moral and intellectual improvement, or they have dressed them like dolls, and used them as toys to amuse their hours of recreation …[1]

Daughters of a southern plantation owner with hundreds of slaves, also a supreme court judge, they threw off their patriarchal heritage and faced barrages of hate for daring, as women, to write and speak publicly: to speak out against their class interests, to speak out against slavery, let alone to speak out for women.

This was the early 1800s. Such questioning of man's right to 'own' everything was unheard of.

At a rally in Philadelphia in 1838, while Sarah Grimké was speaking, an angry mob gathered outside, hurling abuse and rocks. How dare a woman speak publicly! How dare she! As she was hurried out, the hall was burned to the ground.

Not that she was daunted. Here she is in one of her books: 'All I ask of our brethren is, that they will take their feet from off our necks and permit us to stand upright on that ground which God destined us to occupy.'[2]

A surge in agitation for women's rights led in 1848 to the 'Women's Rights Movement' being launched by Elizabeth Cady Stanton, and the 'Declaration of Sentiments' published:

---

1   'Sarah Grimké Calls for Women's Rights, 1838', https://www.ameri canyawp.com/reader/religion-and-reform/sarah-grimke-calls-for-womens-rights-1838/.

2   Ceplair, Larry, *The Public Years of Sarah and Angelina Grimké* (Columbia University Press, New York, 1991), p. 208.

The history of mankind is a history of repeated injuries and usurpations on the part of man toward woman, having in direct object the establishment of an absolute tyranny over her. To prove this, let facts be submitted to a candid world.[3]

The facts being:

- Married women were legally dead in the eyes of the law.

- Women were not allowed to vote.

- Women had to submit to laws when they had no voice in their formation.

- Married women had no property rights.

- Husbands had legal power over and responsibility for their wives to the extent that they could imprison or beat them with impunity.

- Divorce and child custody laws favoured men, giving no rights to women.

- Women had to pay property taxes although they had no representation in the levying of these taxes.

- Most occupations were closed to women and when women did work they were paid only a fraction of what men earned.

---

3   https://www.historyisaweapon.com/defcon1/stantonsent.html.

- Women were not allowed to enter professions such as medicine or law.

- Women had no means to gain an education since no college or university would accept women students.

- With only a few exceptions, women were not allowed to participate in the affairs of the Church.

- Women were robbed of their self-confidence and self-respect, and were made totally dependent on men.

Extraordinarily, virtually a carbon copy of what we were up against in Ireland in 1972. Over 120 years later.

HYENA IN A PETTICOAT

One of the greatest foremothers of them all, Mary Wollstonecraft, was born in London a century before the Grimké
sisters got going in America. Of Irish parentage, Wollstonecraft was fighting for women's rights before the terms 'feminism' or 'feminist' had even been conceived.

Her extraordinary book, *A Vindication of the Rights of
Woman*, published in 1792, was a passionate *cri de coeur*. It
argued that the only way out of the cage women had been
placed in by men, and by society, was via education. Written
in response to what Mary saw as the French Revolution's
betrayal of women under the new constitution, performing
the usual about-turn once the crisis was over, refusing
women full citizenship, the vote, even a proper education, *A
Vindication* was the publishing sensation of the day.

Monsieur Talleyrand, *the* celebrity philosopher/politician
to whom Mary cheekily dedicated *A Vindication*, believed:[1]

Men are destined to live on the stage of the world. A public
education suits them. The paternal home is better for the education of women; they have less need to learn to deal with the

---

1   Wollstonecraft, Mary, *The Vindications. The Rights of Men, The Rights
of Woman* (Broadview Press, New York, 1997) p. 398.

interests of others, than to accustom themselves to a calm and secluded life.

Or here is Rousseau, great papa of *La Révolution*:

[T]he whole education of women ought to be relative to men. To please them, to be useful to them, to make themselves loved and honored by them, to educate them when young, to care for them when grown, to counsel them, to console them and to make life agreeable and sweet to them – these are the duties of women at all times and it should be taught to them from infancy.[2]

Rubbish! believed Wollstonecraft, who argued that until women were properly educated, given the 'tools of reason', they would remain weak and dependent, without agency. She stated that women were 'rendered weak and wretched', especially by a 'false system of education, gathered from the books written on this subject by men who, considering females rather as women than human creatures, have been more anxious to make them [women] alluring mistresses than rational wives'.[3] Education, she believed, was the only way women could 'acquire strength, both of mind and body'

---

2   Flexner, Eleanor and Fitzpatrick, Ellen Frances, *Century of Struggle: The Woman's Rights Movement in the United States* (Harvard University Press, 1996), p. 22.

3   https://www.marxists.org/reference/archive/wollstonecraft-mary/1792/vindication-rights-woman/introduction.htm.

and become independent beings rather than sexual slaves.[4] To marry for support, she said, was legalised prostitution.[5]

In a time when posh ladies sat around in drawing rooms gossiping and feeding sweetmeats to their pooches, and posh men did whatever they wanted, you can just imagine the uproar *A Vindication* created.

At sixteen, Wollstonecraft's ambition was to become a writer and support herself. Beautiful, passionate and luminously intelligent, she packed a bagful into her short life. As a teenager she was often the family breadwinner, spending nights asleep across the door to her mother's bedroom to block her father's drunken rages. Still in her early twenties, she opened her own school, travelled alone to Portugal to nurse her dying friend, and was governess to the daughters of hugely wealthy Anglo-Irish aristocrats Lord and Lady Kingsborough. The daughters were declared crisply by Mary to be 'wild, Irish and unformed', though when she left, fired by Lady Kingsborough allegedly because the daughters had begun to love Mary more than their mother, the eldest declared, 'She (MW) freed my mind of all superstition.'[6] Being sent packing was the catalyst to Mary finding work with the then radical London publisher of the day Joseph Johnson, for whom she became reader, editorial assistant, translator, dinner-party

---

4   *Ibid.*
5   https://www.fff.org/explore-freedom/article/mary-wollstonecraft/.
6   Todd, Janet, *Mary Wollstonecraft: A Revolutionary Life* (Columbia University Press, New York, 2000), p. 116.

guest and, above all, a published and wildly successful author.

In quick succession, she wrote: *A Vindication of the Rights of Men*; *Thoughts on the Education of Daughters*; *Mary: A Fiction*; *Original Stories from Real Life* and *A Vindication of the Rights of Woman*. In 'prose crackling with anger and hope', the publication of the last of these transformed Mary into 'a radical celebrity, famous in progressive circles across Europe and America'.[7]

Tragedy attended the end of her short life; at thirty-two, as she was giving birth to her second – and soon to be equally famous – daughter, Mary Wollstonecraft Shelley, author of *Frankenstein*, Mary's placenta didn't fully disengage. Probably too many medical interventions were made in those pre-antibiotic days, and she died an agonising ten-day death from septicaemia.

An almost worse death was waiting: the death of her reputation when her husband, Godwin, 'with the implacable innocence of a Philosopher of the Truth' (Emily Sunstein) wrote a biography, *A Memoir of the Author of A Vindication of the Rights of Woman*, casually detailing Mary's love liaisons, her out-of-wedlock pregnancy with American love rat Gilbert Imlay in Paris, as well as her radical lifestyle. All hell broke loose – the Establishment finally had a stick to beat what the prime minister of the day's son had dubbed a 'hyena

---

7   https://www.theguardian.com/books/2003/apr/12/featuresreviews.
guardianreview32.

in a petticoat'.

All of her work disappeared, and even friends deserted her, as in the case of Mary Hays, formerly a passionate admirer of Wollstonecraft, who did not include or even mention Mary in her seminal *Female Biography: or Memoirs of Illustrious and Celebrated Women of All Ages and Countries*, such was the opprobrium attaching to Wollstonecraft's name. It wasn't until the suffragettes came on the scene, over a hundred years later, that Mary's name and reputation were retrieved, and she was given her rightful place in feminist literature and history.

Still, as Virginia Woolf wrote in her wonderful 1920s *Common Reader* series:

> [S]he has her revenge. Many millions have died and been forgotten ... since she was buried; and yet as we read her letters and listen to her arguments and consider her experiments, above all, that most fruitful experiment, her relation with Godwin, and realise the high-handed and hot-blooded manner in which she cut her way to the quick of life, one form of immortality is hers undoubtedly: she is alive and active, she argues and experiments, we hear her voice and trace her influence even now among the living.[8]

Oh *Sister*.

---

8   'Four Figures' in Woolf, Virginia, *The Common Reader, Second Series* (Hogarth Press, 1935), http://gutenberg.net.au/ebooks03/0301251h. html.

AMERIKAY

Rather wonderfully, while Mary was being traduced in her country of birth as 'Godwin's lascivious whore' etc., for the early American feminists, including Sarah Grimké, she had become an icon. *A Vindication* was published and re-published in America throughout the nineteenth century, and as generations of American women agitated to gain status and recognition, as the feminist struggle gained traction and became a formal women's rights movement, Wollstonecraft's writings were key.

In 'Making an American Feminist Icon: Mary Wollstonecraft's Reception in US Newspapers, 1800–1869', Eileen Hunt Botting writes:

> Wollstonecraft's name was linked with the most progressive and radical ideas concerning the advancement of women: equal civil and political rights for the sexes; the improvement of female intellectual education; increased economic and professional opportunities for women; new experiments with love, marriage and family life; and the reform of standards of female dress and beauty.[1]

---

1   Hunt Botting, Eileen, 'Making an American Feminist Icon: Mary Wollstonecraft's Reception in US Newspapers, 1800–1869', *History of Political Thought*, Vol. 34, No. 2 (April 2012), https://www.researchgate.net/

She was of course also linked with men's darkest nightmares of what would happen to us ladies if we got ourselves 'educated', with one over-heated author protesting against:

> the moral deformity of those arrogant and audacious, literary, political, philosophical courtesans, who emulous of the fame of Mrs Wollstonecraft have striven to divest the sex of their ancient character … and to invite women to become amazons and statesmen, and directors, and harlots, upon philosophical principles.[2]

Dear oh dear.

Happily the American sisters ignored the over-heated ones and marched on, winning the vote on a draft Equal Rights Amendment for the United States Constitution (1920), to ensure 'Men and women have equal rights throughout the United States', and, under President Kennedy, winning the Civil Rights Act of 1965, prohibiting employment discrimination on the basis of sex, race, religion and national origin. The year 1966 saw the founding of the National Organization for Women, and soon women's groups were springing up everywhere, addressing the needs of black women, white women, Latinas, Asian-Americans, lesbians, women on welfare, businesswomen, professional women and politicians.

Second-wave feminism was on the way.

---

publication/255699166_Making_an_American_Feminist_Icon_Mary_Wollstonecraft's_Reception_in_US_Newspapers_1800-1869.
2   *Ibid.*

THE PILL

The battle for contraception and the arrival of the contraceptive pill, of course, changed everything.

One of the ways, historically, men had gained power over women and grabbed the high ground, was because women became pregnant, and once pregnant had to leave the public sphere to look after the children. And of course those were the lucky ones – women and girls who got pregnant 'outside of wedlock' were universally excoriated, thrown out of their families, out of their villages, often out of life itself.

Attempts by us humans to enjoy the pleasures of sex with one another while at the same time thwarting pregnancy go back to the beginnings of time. Potions, lotions, leaves, stones, honey, acacia leaves, acacia gum, lint, pomegranate, date palm, myrrh, rue, willow, artemisia, silphium, penny-royal, halves of lemon, crocodile dung, lead, mercury – what haven't women used to prevent pregnancy, often at great risk to their own health, even of death?

In America, in the early 1900s, an extraordinary young woman, Nurse Margaret Sangar, whose own mother (both her parents were Irish Catholics – her father's family fled from the famine) endured fourteen pregnancies and died aged forty from tuberculosis, had become horrified at the endless pregnancies and botched backstreet abortions endured by the poor and immigrant women she worked among in New York. As a result, she began a lifelong campaign for effective, reliable and affordable birth control for all women. She was jailed, vilified and slandered throughout her life – she still is among right-wing groups in America – but Margaret Sangar's dream of an effective and, crucially, affordable birth control pill came to fruition in 1960 when, thanks to funding from another woman, wealthy philanthropist Katharine McCormick, Sangar's 'pill' was licensed by the US Food & Drug Administration and released onto the market.

Even in Sangar's time, upper- and middle-class women had access to private abortion and to whatever the latest form of contraception was – early condoms for the guys or crude diaphragms for the ladies – but the pill was the first almost 100-per-cent-reliable method of birth control available to, and affordable for, all.

It was instrumental in changing everything.

The uptake in America was spectacular. Women got the message, though in those early days many women had to go to extreme lengths to hide the pill from the men in their lives, but the advantages of not 'falling' pregnant every year usually outweighed the risks. Here was something that gave women control over whether or not they got pregnant, something that worked. It changed 'sexual politics' forever. Suddenly women could decide if they wanted to delay marriage, delay starting a family, not start a family at all, not get married at all. Quite suddenly they were free.

As the Women's Movement took hold, as women surged into third-level education, the workforce and the professions, took lovers, bought bikinis and decided there was more to life – a lot more – than settling down in a house in the 'burbs, with the gadgets, it was clear that the pill had helped to change everything. For women. And for men. The American sisters made sure it did.

SIMONE AND BETTY AND
SIGMUND AND STOKELY

In 1963 American author Betty Friedan published *The Feminine Mystique*. Starting out with the idea of writing a magazine article checking up on how her ex-college mates from Smith College were getting on now that they had supposedly hit the holy grail of matrimony, husband, kiddies, home and, oh the excitement, domestic appliances, Friedan found to her surprise that most of them were unaccountably miserable. They had been educated enough to know that being an unpaid domestic slave for the rest of their lives didn't amount to life's jackpot.

They were a generation caught between the eroding of patriarchy's grip, and the post-war, women-get-back-in-the-kitchen shtick. Or, Perfect Wives in Perfect Homes, with lantern-jawed men sitting at their leisure with newspapers, pipes and food to hand, while 'the little woman' rushed around in her frilly pinny making sure everyone was happy, clean, fed, watered, cared for. With a smile. Always with a smile.

Looking back, it's amazing the effort put into mythologising this bullshit – everything from government propaganda to magazines (all then edited by men), to education. A woman's place was in the home and that was bloody well that.

Sigmund Freud, that wonderful champion of human sanity, wrote of women's roles:

> I believe that all reforming action in law and education would break down in front of the fact that, long before the age at which a man can earn a position in society, Nature has determined woman's destiny through beauty, charm, and sweetness. Law and custom have much to give women that has been withheld from them, but the position of women will surely be what it is: in youth an adored darling and in mature years a loved wife.[1]

Jaysus Sigmund, check your prejudices.

In *The Feminine Mystique*, Friedan used many of the ideas developed by Simone de Beauvoir, a contemporary of Freud, in her 1949 stomping masterpiece *The Second Sex*, but laid them out via the suffocating realities of educated, middle-class, white American women.

De Beauvoir's existential howl of fury – that women are invisible, enslaved and subordinate to men, always the 'other' never the 'one' – sold 22,000 copies on its first day of publication and has gone on selling since, becoming the intellectual treatise par excellence on women's oppression. Her characterisation of women as societally powerless and

---

1   Morales, Maria (ed.), *Mill's, The Subjection of Women: Critical Essays* (Rowman & Littlefield, Maryland, 2005), p. 15.

invisible didn't just strike a chord; it struck entire orchestras. Here was a woman fearlessly, brilliantly and thrillingly lancing the sacred bulls; take that Pythagoras, Freud, Engels, Shakespeare and Edgar Allan Poe.

Men, argued de Beauvoir, or 99.9 per cent of them, viewed women as 'not men' and therefore not autonomous or even capable of autonomy. Over human evolution, through this 'othering' of women and traditional motherhood, which left woman 'riveted to her body' like an animal, men had seized all of the high ground – the means of production, control of finances, access to learning and a million other things; a tactic used for millennia to enforce control by one group over another.

You know the story. We are great. You, the 'other', are less great. We are Aryans. You, the 'others', are scum. We are Christians. You 'the others' are Muslim. And so on and so on.

It was only by rejecting the definition of themselves by men, by the patriarchy, by redefining themselves, taking control of their destinies, their lives, their bodies and sexuality, their agency in the world, that women could grow up, stop being infantilised by the patriarchy and become fully autonomous human beings.

Hundreds of thousands of French women agreed. *The Second Sex*, in a newly revised edition (2005), continues to sell millions of copies worldwide.

As Betty Friedan's withering takedown of the lot, offered

to modern, educated women, gained a larger audience in America, women's groups began to spring up everywhere.

By the mid-1960s many female activists in the Civil Rights Movement, black and white, were fed up with being cast as girlfriends, tea makers, leafleteers and gun-toters for the big boys. Being chosen as the girlfriend of a handsome male civil rights activist was sexier than being a typist or a suburban housewife, but you were still playing second fiddle, still ignoring what you needed as a woman.

For many of the early second wavers it was the often blatant misogyny of the male organisers that drove them to fight for their own liberation. At the famous 'Dialectics of Liberation' conference in the Roundhouse in London in 1967, Stokely Carmichael, hero of the Black Power Movement, was asked what women's position should be in the revolution. 'Horizontal,' was the sneering reply.

Caroline Coon, artist and lifelong London-based activist and feminist, was at that Roundhouse conference. When I asked her about it, she wrote:

[E]ven today that Stokely Carmichael moment at the Roundhouse in 1967 strikes me with dread, as a big wake-up moment and one that galvanised women in the 1970s into organising 'separately' from the male-dominated political Left … it was one of those sexist psychic shocks that I have seen, over all these years, propel each new generation of young women forward as they realise they have to unbury the history of feminism over and over again. Hurray for today's #MeToo and #TimesUp![2]

The second wavers passionately believed in 'unburying'. Everything, but everything, of a woman's life had to be interrogated: the relationship between the sexes, the 'nuclear' family, access to the labour market, equal pay, lesbianism, rape. Oh yes, rape – whatever we wear, wherever we go, Yes means Yes and No means No.

There was the invasion of the 'Miss America' contest – 'a meat market utterly degrading to women'. A sheep was symbolically crowned and women arrived in busloads to protest, theatrically burning items deemed degrading and irrelevant to liberated women's lives – six-inch stilettos, girdles (yes, everyone wore them then), padded bras, make-up, etc., in a 'freedom bin'.

In the days that followed, women came out as cheerfully lesbian on primetime television, a beautiful young Kate Millett proudly proclaiming, 'It's women for me from now on!' You could almost hear the patriarchy gasp: *What?* Women liking women? What's to become of us?

Most importantly of all, hours-long consciousness-raising sessions became the rage.

---

2   Email correspondence, November 2019.

CONSCIOUSNESS RAISING

Consciousness raising essentially grew out of 'radicalism' in New York; those who believed the only way to change was to get to the root cause of a problem, and that the key to successful change was 'raising your consciousness' or becoming aware of oppression in your own life; becoming aware, or 'woke' as the young people call it now.

Everybody who was seriously into the movement took part in consciousness raising – arguably the most personal, the most political and the most life-changing act of all.

The New York feminists took consciousness raising to another level. Early feminist groups sometimes consisted of hundreds of women, but mostly consciousness-raising groups were small, intimate gatherings of ten, fifteen women in someone's living room. There were rules. Nobody was to play hostess. This was about changing the world, specifically changing the patriarchal world, and serving up finger foods and quiche was NOT part of the deal. Also, nobody was in charge. The core of the movement was egalitarianism. An egalitarianism that was in direct opposition to patriarchy with its endless power stratifications, its endless cycle of domination and submission. As Kate Millett said in Vanessa Engle's brilliant series of 2010 documentaries, *Women*, for BBC Four, if we have a head someone can come along and chop that head off, but if we are all equal, silencing us is more difficult.

In sessions everyone had an equal right to speak. And there were to be *no* men. Women, the early sisters argued, had been systematically separated from each other by the patriarchy, imprisoned in the patriarchy's belief that it was right and proper for men to rule the world and for women to serve men while they were doing so, and a man at a meeting was likely, just because of his sex, and because of patriarchy's history, to take over the show. The women were damned if they were going to put up with that. Consciousness raising was their safe space, a space women desperately needed to examine their oppression, to get to the root of it, the why of it and, from there, the how to change it. If men wanted to liberate themselves, let them go and set up their own consciousness-raising groups. It's strange how few men did, or have done so since.

At the core of consciousness raising was the belief that in the personal *was* the political. That everything that women had been propagandised to believe were personal problems – their appearance, the division of household labour, sex, marriage, divorce, childcare, access to contraception and abortion, access to education – were actually political problems, the political realities of living under a patriarchy. Raising issues from a single woman's personal experience to a shared public and political experience meant the issues could be challenged and changed.

Why do we smile so much? Why are we so afraid of our anger? Why do we dress to please? Why *don't* we have contraception and abortion? Why *don't* we have equal pay?

As June Levine wrote in *Sisters*: 'the question most often asked was my old favourite, *why?* ... Why did we hate ourselves, distrust ourselves, distrust each other?'[1]

As radical feminist Heidi Hartmann wrote in 'The Unhappy Marriage of Feminism and Marxism': 'Women's discontent ... is not the neurotic lament of the maladjusted, but a response to a social structure in which women are systematically dominated, exploited, and oppressed.'[2]

Under a patriarchy women were isolated, either inside a patriarchal nuclear family or inside a patriarchal workplace, and made to believe the problems they faced in their lives were peculiar to them. Through consciousness raising, women began to realise they were not mad, not neurotic, not over-demanding, impossible-to-satisfy hysterics, but, like thousands of other women, battling unmanageable restrictions.

As Kathie Sarachild of the early radical women's group in New York wrote in 1973, consciousness raising was about 'studying the whole gamut of women's lives, starting with the full reality of one's own'.[3]

---

1   Levine (2009), p. 144.
2   Hartmann, Heidi I., 'The Unhappy Marriage of Marxism and Feminism', p. 10, https://web.ics.purdue.edu Hartmann_1979.
3   Sarachild, Kathie, 'Consciousness-Raising: A Radical Weapon', in

The blowback, from radical men as well as the mainstream, was pretty intense. Consciousness raising was dismissed as petty, self-indulgent, bourgeois, *personal*. Consciousness-raising groups were 'bitch fests'. Consciousness raising was just 'therapy' for middle-class women, nothing to do with 'the struggle'. Consciousness-raising groups were 'coffee cabals'.

Wrong, wrong, wrong, argued the women. Consciousness raising was and is the ultimate tool for interrogating the politics of women's lives and out of that provoking a mass movement of awakened women who will not be bought off with single-issue wins or small concessions; a movement built from the ground up, built on one's lived reality, not built on studying books, or the struggles of others.

As Malcolm X wrote at the time:

> [I]f you give people a thorough understanding of what it is that confronts them, and the basic causes that produce it, they'll create their own program; and when the people create a program you get action.[4]

Feminist Revolution: An Abridged Edition (Random House, New York, 1978), https://www.rapereliefshelter.bc.ca/learn/resources/consciousness-raising-radical-weapon-kathie-sarachild.

4 Malcolm X at the Audubon Ballroom, 20 December 1964, http://malcolmxfiles.blogspot.com/2013/07/at-audubon-ballroom-december-20-1964.html.

KATE MILLETT AND THE
'LAVENDER MENACE'

Women's movements – suffragettes, women's rights organisations, 'women's libbers', Repeal the Eighth activists – have one goal: improving the lives of women. Many of the women involved in these movements have made enormous personal sacrifices, taken huge risks to push the cause of 'les femmes' forward. Kate Millett, one of the inimitable founding sisters of second-wave feminism, was one such activist. She died of a heart attack in Paris, aged eighty-three, on a bright morning in September 2017, bent almost double with arthritis over her walking frame, her partner of many years by her side. She had been about to attend a conference on her heroine Simone de Beauvoir: her commitment to 'the cause' shone out undimmed. Hurray!

She was the daughter of Irish-American parents. Her father was an alcoholic who beat his wife and kids, then abandoned them; her mum was the one who supported the family. Millett, a brilliant scholar, was sent off to Oxford funded by an aunt and was the first American woman to graduate with first-class honours there. Later she said the most important thing she did at Oxford was to read, and absorb, de Beauvoir's masterpiece, *The Second Sex*.

Married, she returned to New York and radical feminist

politics, part of the second wavers when there were only fifteen of them in New York. Imagine, *fifteen*!

Chucked out of her teaching post in Barnard for supporting student demonstrations, she took up an abandoned
dissertation and began 'working furiously'. Like de Beauvoir, she was hugely well read and took on the then heroes
of the Left, the self-styled 'sexual revolutionaries' – D. H.
Lawrence, Henry Miller, Norman Mailer, with Mr Freud
getting a good pummelling along the way for his 'penis envy'
nonsense – and began interrogating what they were actually
saying.

Their writings, Millett believed, were reiterating, in
modern guise, the endless domination/subjugation themes
of male literature, and their prose – with its objectification of
women, a reduction of them to the sexual gratification men
could get from (usually) violently 'penetrating' them as they,
the women, supposedly gagged on a twenty-four-hour basis
for the mighty phallus – was nasty, vicious and indicative of
a virulent sexism.

Misogyny, not liberation, was at the new literature's
core. Far from being the 'sexual revolutionaries' they liked
to be seen as, Millett deemed them 'counter-revolutionaries',
doing the patriarchy's dirty work.

It's so obvious now, but back then the Left was so busy
fighting censorship it seemed happy to ignore what these
guys were actually writing about, what they were actually
saying about women.

British feminist Sheila Jeffreys goes further. She believes not even Kate Millett could have foreseen how the publication – and therefore legitimisation – by reputable publishing houses of the works of Lawrence, Miller, Mailer *et al.*, with their deeply misogynistic portrayals of women, would open the door to the legitimisation, and proliferation, of pornography.

In *Sexual Politics*, Millett wrote of a relationship between the sexes that was institutionalised, a form of 'interior colonisation', an oppression 'sturdier than any form of segregation, and more rigorous than class stratification'.[1]

She added, 'However muted its appearance may be, sexual dominion obtains nevertheless as perhaps the most pervasive ideology of our culture and provides its most fundamental concept of power.'

Millett said she'd listened back 'rhapsodically' to early versions: 'it was a fiery little speech directed at girls, witty and tart and stuff like that – at least I thought it was … It needed a job of editing but at the time I thought it was glorious.'[2]

Glorious it was. And thousands upon thousands of women, and men, thought it was too. Print run after print run sold out. Totally unprepared, Millett was shoved into the limelight, anointed a spokesperson for the Women's

---

1   Millett, Kate, *Sexual Politics* (Columbia University Press, New York, 2016), p. 2.
2   *The New Yorker*, 7 September 2017.

Movement, had her portrait on the cover of *Time* magazine, and was in demand everywhere.

Initially fame was 'amusing', but it quickly turned dark. Millett said a 'ruin of interviews, articles, attacks' wore her down; 'it grew tedious, an indignity', she wrote in *Flying* (1974). 'Never get too famous,' she said in Vanessa Engle's BBC Four three-part documentary *Women*, which aired in March 2010, 'then you're just a mark and everyone shoots at you.'

A personal crisis added to the drama. The fact that she now identified as bisexual made her stance difficult to maintain. As Millett wrote later, 'The line goes, inflexible as a fascist edict, that bisexuality is a cop-out.'

She was painfully 'outed' at a meeting at Columbia University. 'Are you a lesbian? Say it. Are you?' yelled an activist in the audience. 'Five hundred people looking at me,' Millett wrote. 'Everything pauses, faces look up in terrible silence. I hear them not breathe. That word in public, the word I waited half a lifetime to hear. Finally I am accused. "Say it. Say you are a lesbian!"'[3]

Millett remembered how academics then went round saying, 'Oh my God, she's a queer, everything she wrote before must be nonsensical.'

These days, thanks to women like Kate Millett, coming

---

3   AP News.com, 7 September 2017, https://apnews.com/3987f43f-58174dcaaeb8ce7f81fbca0f.

out as a lesbian is entirely different. Back then, lesbians were looked on with disfavour, even within the Women's Movement. Known disparagingly as the 'lavender menace', they were deemed a threat to the movement's 'respectability'. Millett found it saddening and deeply hypocritical. She thought the societal lie that gender stereotypes are natural rather than cultural had to be endlessly challenged for women to gain their freedom. 'There is no way out of such a dilemma but to rebel and be broken, [be] stigmatized and cured.'[4]

Millett herself was thoroughly broken. Following fame and fortune, she had a breakdown. The usual hospital treatment with pills and labels ensued. There was even an extraordinary sojourn in Ireland, where, at Mary Robinson's invitation, she'd come to address the Labour Party but got arrested at Shannon Airport after suffering a nervous collapse. She was checked into the local loony bin from which she was miraculously rescued by activist and feminist Margaretta D'Arcy on the grounds that she would be given 'a safe house'. Ivor Browne signed her out and in stepped Nell McCafferty, then running 'an open house' in Dublin. Her descriptions of a still very manic Millett blasting along on cocktails, liquid lunches and astronomically expensive transatlantic calls to Amerikay are wonderful. Afterwards

---

4   Mead, Rebecca, 'Postscript: Kate Millett's Radical Spirit', *The New Yorker*, 7 September 2017, https://www.newyorker.com/books/page-turner/postscript-kate-millets-radical-spirit.

Millett wrote a sweet letter, apologising for being a pain in the neck. 'Everything flew asunder because of manic outrage … my fault to have been crazed – never mind that you're sane and sober, and remembering it.'[5]

Back home in the feminists/artists colony she'd founded with her money from *Sexual Politics* and where she grew Christmas trees – a crop she reckoned even disorganised artists could probably raise without killing – she wrote and lectured, but sadly spent many years isolated and almost forgotten. *Sexual Politics* was out of print until very recently (2016), when it was republished by Columbia with a forward by Rebecca Mead of *The New Yorker*, making it available to a whole new, eager audience.

Kate Millett wrote nine other books, but *Sexual Politics* remains the one for which she is best known. As friend and fellow feminist Andrea Dworkin wrote in 2003, 'The world was sleeping and Kate Millett woke it up.'[6]

That she managed to stay alive herself until the grand old age of eighty-three is remarkable. No martyr to the cause, she loved life. Remembering the early, heady days of resistance, she wrote:

> The happiness of those times, the joy of participation, the excitement of being part of my own time, of living on the edge,

---

5   McCafferty, Nell, *Nell* (Gardners Books, London, 2004), pp. 332–5.
6   *The New Statesman*, 14 July 2003.

of being so close to events you can almost intuit them. To raise one's voice in protest, just as the protest is expressed in life, in the streets, in relationships and friendships. Then, in a moment of public recognition, the face of the individual becomes a woman's face ...[7]

Now that America is being fronted by what John Cleese dubbed 'an extraordinary caricature of an asshole', it's easy to forget how we once looked up to America[8] – Land of the Free – where all the good stuff originated, such as jazz, rock and roll, Elvis, the Twist, chewing gum, Aretha Franklin, Coke, civil rights, JFK, Jackie Kennedy Onassis, RFK, Martin Luther King, hippies and second-wave feminism. America was the crucible in which exciting things were birthed and if the American sisters hadn't got fed up toting guns, making tea, rolling joints, typing manifestos, etc., for the male marchers, would second-wave feminism have kicked off so dramatically? It was their experience in civil rights agitations that informed their view on how women's liberation should, and would, take place. It was their radical take on politics, their insight into how consciousness raising liberates from the inside out and that replacing patriarchal

---

7   From Kate Millett's acceptance speech when inducted into the National Women's Hall of Fame in 2013.

8   https://www.thedailybeast.com/monty-pythons-john-cleese-and-eric-idle-on-50-years-of-flying-circus-and-the-trump-and-brexit-shitshow?ref=home&via=twitterpage.

power structures with female ones was no liberation at all, that laid the groundwork for so much of what developed over here.

One can only hope that the 'extraordinary caricature of an asshole', who has so divided America and unleashed so much brutal misogyny, hatred and racism, will soon be replaced, and a kinder, less bloated, less hideous and cooler America will re-emerge.

DISAPPEARING
FEMINISM

SECTION V

ON OUR KNEES AND CONNEMARA

Back in my own life, back in the 1970s, I'd left *The Irish Press* and moved back home after the IWLM fizzled. I remember just Mum and me in the big old house, though maybe that's sibling rivalry and I've neatly excised all my other siblings from the picture. Still, I remember Mum upstairs in the drawing room with a coffee, *The Irish Times* and one biscuit, her three weekly books from the RDS library on the little table beside her, her little dog at her feet and me down in the basement bashing away happily on my portable green Olivetti. I was writing my first book, *On Our Knees* ('the great are only great because we are on our knees' – James Larkin), a look at Ireland in the 1970s.

Happy days.

In the evenings Mum cooked supper and I brought her up that day's pages. She was a good editor, intervening only when my self-righteous, twenty-something self went off at an uncontrollable gallop.

On Our Knees was helped to realisation by the legendary Maureen Cleave of the *Evening Standard*, famous for her interview with (her friends) The Beatles in which John Lennon pronounced: 'We're bigger than Jesus.' Cue terrific furore. Maureen persuaded literary agent Nicholas Thompson to take me on. Nicholas, then living in splendour in Pont Street, near Belgravia, was also agent to writer James Cameron and immediately threw a supper party to introduce his newest catch, Ms Wild Oirish. Within weeks he had a contract and a tiny advance from Pan Books to do the book, and here I was – a writer!

My inamorato, now more or less accepted by the family despite Dad's total opposition when he was alive, had gone ahead to Africa. Blue aerogrammes, tiny writing crammed top to bottom and side to side, arrived every second day – 'I love you, I can't wait to have you here, I want you,' etc., etc.

Manuscript complete, I delivered it to Pan in London and headed off to L'Afrique in a dress a friend had dramatically taken off and given to me at a going-away party at Big Sis's house the night before.

Shamefully, I don't remember buying Mum so much as a bottle of wine as a thank you.

Africa! That unforgettable blast of oven heat when the plane doors open, the tiny one-storey airport shimmering in the furnace, the cerulean blue of the Indian Ocean with ludicrously photogenic palm trees clack-clacking along the shore. The shock of the gated 'expat' communities by the sea, while thousands of Tanzanians subsisted in suffocating tin shacks outside of town. The roads were thick with traffic, pedestrians, the men in spotlessly white lungis, the women in brilliantly coloured kangas, all of them filing slowly past either side in the baking heat, the shops with their 1950s goods, the bars along the coast with cement floors, plastic chairs, palm tree roofs, delicious snacks, ice-cold beers.

I got a job as a reporter on *The Daily News*, the English-language paper. I got tanked on Konyagi, the local gin, fell off my little motorbike with shock the first time I encountered a gecko the size of a dog. As fresh meat in the enclosed expat world I was a hit. I wore my feminism like a bright badge and was my inamorato's pride and joy: his young, Irish, feminist revolutionary.

In the early mornings I wrote my first novel, *Fathers Come First*, republished as a 'modern classic' by The Lilliput Press in 2015. There I sat in our United Nations Development Programme bungalow in my bikini in the boiling heat, trusty little Olivetti on a bare desk, fronds of bougainvillea tapping at the window. Outside, I heard the kronk of an African crow, sand creaking under the postman's huge black bike, a snake on the porch, all while I wrote of Ireland, a convent boarding school, nuns, grey skies, frigid winters, finding a boyfriend, getting rid of a boyfriend.

Evenings were with friends – Tanzanian, Kenyan, South African, English, Canadian, American, Russian. We got involved with the socialists then working at the university, 'How Europe Underdeveloped Africa', the 'Small is Beautiful' projects run along lines beloved of Ernst Schumacher, the Ujamaa films project being run in the villages by Gary and Paula Belkin. A lot of time was spent staying in a friend's beach house up the coast, hot sand fronting on to the Indian Ocean, a glittering blue silk scarf stretching to the horizon.

I had an IUD fitted. 'Your wife [yes, we got married weeks after I arrived in Africa] has a very low pain threshold', the doctor told my man, while I, in agony, suppressed my rage. How would you like a wire trap shoved up your wedding tackle Mr Doctor Man? My man developed malaria the next day and we lay side by side in the heat, the blinds pulled, he on one side of the bed saying, 'My head feels as if there's a Kilner jar in it rolling from side to side,' me on the other, moaning, 'God, oh God, oh God.' My man saying he thinks his temperature is going over 104. Me staggering to the phone to ring the English doctor, who's had a few too many Konyagis. 'Put him in a bucket of cold water,' says Doc, thinking I'm talking about the dog.

On the stereo, shipped out from London by the Foreign Office, we play Miriam Makeba, Miles Davis, Nina Simone, Hugh Masekela and Joni Mitchell, the frogs outside barking their chorus into the dark velvet night.

He takes me to visit an old girlfriend, the (white) widow of a freedom fighter. At first she's kind. Then, after mucho vino, she insists I try on a red dress of hers, making me twirl in front of him. 'Isn't it gorgeous? Doesn't it look fabulous on her?' As we're leaving she asks for the dress back. Thumping home in the jeep over pitted dirt roads he is furious. How dare she! What a terrible thing to do! I don't mind. The dress wasn't really me and anyway, I thought, she must be desperate. She's an old one. Who cares what she thinks? She was forty-six.

Disaster came unexpectedly. While he was away on safari I had a weekend fling. Lovely. I even told him about it when he got home. Well, he never stopped telling me of the affairs he'd had when he lived in Africa with his first wife; sauce for the goose, yummy for the gander, go I.

He didn't take the news well, and a ferocious row ensued.

Then, that night, he opened up about some things that happened in his childhood. I was so tired after all the shouting and whiskey and tears that I kept falling asleep. Outraged, he kept prodding me awake: 'I'm telling you the most important things of my life and you're sleeping!'

Can we talk about it in the morning?

We were what I think is deemed 'enmeshed'. We loved each other. We wanted to dissolve into each other. We wanted to be each other. We hated each other. We wanted to hate each other.

His potent chat-up shtick was very much along the lines of: 'Won't you come into my parlour?' as the spider said to the fly. Loads of flattery. Loads of looks. Loads of mood. By the time, intrigued, I'd wandered in to have a closer look, the web had fallen tight around me; big, naïve schoolgirl without a clue who I really was, I wanted his web tight around me. I mistook my need to be wanted as love.

Days after my 'confession', he began an affair with a visiting journalist. Of course she was blonde, gorgeous, witty and, worst of all, ironic. He gave her my bikini and took her to our favourite beach. Three days passed and then our film producer friend Gary Belkin drove me over to the bungalow, told Madame to sling her hook and left us to sort things out.

A week later I got on a plane back to London. A pattern began. Whenever things got so bad that I left, a few days later, abandoning job, house, goods, etc., he would follow. We ended up back in London with Big Sis and her husband. From London we headed out to Mexico, his next assignment. Then it was on down to Honduras; the year after that, 1974, to Peru, with me canoeing up the Amazon with a Jesuit priest to an Indian river village, and later, travelling by bus to Bolivia. Every year we flew back to London, staying with Big Sis and her husband, visiting Mum and sisters in Dublin, visiting friends on the way who'd 'come back' from Africa, now trapped in airless flats with huge dogs, dull-coated and dull-eyed, the central heating roaring, grey air, grey skies pressing in at the windows. Having come home for schools for the kids, come home to find a home, to buy a house in the suburbs, to stop being an expat, they looked as trapped, as diminished, as their dogs.

In each country he was assigned to, I worked also. As a freelance journalist. As a reporter for Concern and Oxfam. As a photographer. Still, as I was cut off from the company of feminist friends and peers back at home, always 'the young one' amidst the usually older and deeply conservative expat community, my feminist politics didn't develop; they stayed frozen around a few catchphrases without any analysis of the situation I was in – the wife, without power, of a powerful male.

By 1979 it was decided I should come back to Ireland, get a job, find a home, preferably not in the suburbs. In the meantime, he would stay with Big Sis and her husband and get some temporary work at the Foreign Office in London. He started missing weekends home. I rang Big Sis. Was he up to something? 'No smoke without fire,' Big Sis hinted.

I broke it off with him, upped sticks and went to live in Connemara, wrote *On Our Backs: Sexual Attitudes in 1970s Ireland*, and had a passionate affair with an older writer. Oh joy!

We lived in a tiny stone cottage, the big, crumpled Paul Henry blue mountains of Connemara all around us, the sea an insane lapis lazuli blue, skirts of obsidian-coloured seaweed slapping against the little stone pier, the fishermen at the bar, their huge hands around pints of Guinness – the 'singing stones' we called them as, without preamble, they broke into *sean-nós*. How could such heartbreaking sounds come from these men of granite?

He said my writing was 'stilted'. 'You should write like you speak, Peteen.' I read everything he wrote and didn't say anything. The complexity of it! He said, 'No matter what job you are asked to do – a book review or a novel – you give it everything.' He had been a friend of Samuel Beckett and once asked him what was it about James Joyce that made him so brilliant. 'Ferocious dedication to the task in hand' was the wonderful reply. My lover's book reviews, of impossibly difficult European writers I'd never heard of, took four to five days, the typed finished pages sent off by mail from the cupboard-sized post office across the sound. My book reviews took an evening, cross-legged in front of the turf fire, wind roaring down the chimney, bottle of wine at the ready, publisher's PR to hand.

When my lover left to go back to his wife and children – oh yes, I'm sorry to say my feminism didn't stop me there – I went through hell.

HOW COME YOUR FEMINISM DISAPPEARS
WHEN YOU MOST NEED IT?

As if by magic, Prince Charming reappeared on the horizon. We decided to try again. This time it was to be new marriage, new wedding rings, new vows, new house in the Wicklow mountains, new life, babies. By now my feminism had disappeared to such an extent that when, in 1982, the *Sunday Independent* sent me out for review June Levine's wonderful book *Sisters*, about her life and the story of the Women's Movement, I was snippy about it.

Juno! My wonderful friend, wonderful co-founder of the IWLM, Juno who'd thanked me warmly in her dedication, who came up to visit, bringing chocolates, flowers and wine, and here I was being snippy about her book, making jokes about it, amusing the men.

Juno, who a few years later probably – no, definitely – saved my life. The day I was supposed to make up my mind about travelling back to Africa with my man and the babies, his plan being to set us up in a house there while he, ever so conveniently, would travel back and forth without me to London.

Of course I was suspicious, but under intense pressure to agree.

Then June rang and, when she heard what was going on,

said in that special voice she had when about to deliver one of her heat-seeking missiles:

> Please tell me, that you are not *completely* mad. That you are not going to let that bastard take you and the children to somewhere thousands of miles from your friends and family while he travels backwards and forwards to London?

It was just the missile I needed. Thank you Juno! No to Africa. No to Prince Charming and his laughably see-through plans.

I stayed put.

A LOVE(ETT) CHILD

The Ireland I stayed in was of course still doing ghastly things to young girls. And despite the Catholic Church's best efforts, every few years hypocrisy's smooth landscape was violently disturbed, the upheaval usually involving 'women's issues', or yet another female martyred on hypocrisy and patriarchy's altar.

In 1984, a month before my own tiny daughter was born, it was Ann Lovett's turn to be sacrificed.

Ann Lovett was a fifteen-year-old schoolgirl when she gave birth alone, out of doors, on a freezing winter's day in January 1984 at the foot of a statue of the Virgin Mary in a small Irish town. By the time she was found she was already travelling fast into irreversible shock, her baby dead, wrapped in her school coat on a stone beside her.

She had been fourteen when she became pregnant, fifteen when she took a scissors to cut the umbilical cord, left her school, the inaptly named 'Convent of Mercy', early, and instead of going home to have lunch with her younger sister Patricia, as she always did, went to a friend's house. Ann asked her friend to 'come out' with her, but the friend said she couldn't, she was minding the house. Ann asked her for a cigarette, then left. She walked up the long, steep main street of Granard, Co. Longford, to her most pitiful Golgotha, a stone grotto alongside the granite colossus – the Catholic Church – that looms over the town. There, under the statue of Our Lady of Lourdes, beside the kneeling statue of St Bernadette, ironically a girl about her own age, she laboured alone and in the now driving wind and rain of that bitter January evening, and gave birth to a full-term baby boy, weighing six pounds three ounces, strangled during birth by the umbilical cord.

Perhaps an hour later two schoolboys discovered her. Passing by the grotto on their way back from school they noticed a red schoolbag thrown into the side of the little lane leading to the grotto and 'heard moaning'. The two boys ran to get the help of a nearby farmer.

'A little girl is after falling.'

'Who is she?'

'Ann Lovett.'

The farmer thought the 'little girl' had fallen from the top of the grotto. When he came with the boys he said she was 'very cold'. Her eyes were 'opening and closing'. Her school uniform was soaking and she was covered in blood. The farmer hurried up to the priest's house close by. The priest said: 'It's a doctor you need, not a priest.' The farmer stood his ground. 'We need you too, Father. The baby is dead and the little girl might be dying too.'[1]

---

1   SCANNAL, 'The Story of Ann Lovett', aired 27 September 2004. https://www.youtube.com/watch?v=-LRvNDt4QII.

Reports vary as to what happened next. It seems the priest, at the farmer's insistence, came to the grotto to give the little girl and her baby the Last Rites. Another neighbour called an ambulance and came with blankets. Finally, the local GP, Ann's father Diarmuid and her youngest brother arrived, and Ann and her baby were taken by car to her parents' house on the Main Street and from there by ambulance to Mullingar. Over two hours had passed since the boys had found her and her 'grand little lad'. Within twenty minutes of arriving at the hospital she was dead. The gardaí said they were not called until three-and-a-half hours later, when one of them, coming on late duty, said he'd heard rumours 'there'd been an abortion' in the town.

The small town, population 1,120, was just 'getting back to normal' when a man, reportedly one of the gardaí, broke silence and rang one of the Sunday papers. 'Something terrible has happened.'

The story, titled 'Young Girl Dies in Field After Giving Birth', was read out as part of the next morning's papers at the end of *The Late Late Show*: 'Young girl dies in field after giving birth, my goodness me …' said Gay Byrne, the show's host, then chucked the paper on the floor with 'Nothing terribly exciting there.'[2]

As an example of the male callousness of the time it was appalling, but as a newsman who prided himself on

2   *Ibid.*

having his finger on the nation's pulse, 'Gaybo' couldn't have been more wrong. The death of Ann Lovett and her baby convulsed Ireland for months.

Why had a little girl become so isolated that she'd given birth, on her own, in a grotto on a foul winter evening? Who was the father of the child? Where was he? Where were her parents? Who were her friends? Where were they? What about the nuns and the teachers at her convent school? In the days when all schoolgirls were whip thin, had they not noticed *anything*? Who was the family's GP? What about the townspeople of Granard who presumably saw her on her last terrible journey up to the grotto, walking up the main street in her school uniform, about to give birth, scissors in her pocket? Had nobody seen *anything*?

The more questions were asked, the more tight-lipped the people of Granard became. Reporters and journalists were told to 'Fuck off! Fuck away off ye parasites!', forbidden from talking to friends of Ann, yelled at in the bar of the local hotel: 'If any daughter of mine got pregnant I'd give her such a "root up the arse" she'd never do it again.'

Extraordinarily, the 'hostile silence', the 'nobody knew anything' position, which was backed by Church and State, held for thirty-two years.

Here are some facts about the case:

- The coroner's report, apart from the one bald statement, 'Death due to irreversible shock caused by haemorrhage and exposure during childbirth', has never been published.

- The police report has never been published.

- The Department of Health and Education's report, employers of Ann Lovett's teachers, has never been published.

- In State papers released in 2016, a journalist from *The Irish Times* found a slim file containing the following: firstly, a series of cuttings from newspaper reports at the time. Secondly, a brief handwritten note, dated 7 February 1984, which read 'Government received a report from Minister for Health and Education; expressed sympathy with the parents and family; in so far as an inquiry is concerned, there will be an inquest', adding 'great personal tragedy which should not be compounded by particular kinds of attention'. And, a short note dated 10 February, which read: 'The minister for health mentioned certain further facts which had come to light since his first report. The course of action to be followed by him was agreed.'

- In a documentary for TG4, the editor of the local newspaper, *The Longford Leader*, said he knew nothing about the girl. Or her baby. He first heard about it on RTÉ radio. His paper led the next day with the following headline: 'Granard Nuns did not know girl was pregnant.'

- As Rosita Boland notes in her excellent story about Ann Lovett thirty-four years later, 'Extensive efforts by *The Irish Times* to determine what, if any, archival documents relating to Ann Lovett are held in the Departments of Health, Justice, or Education, have yielded no results. Nor have inquiries to the Garda press office.'

- 'Rural Ireland was a closed society then on matters relating to the care and protection of children,' Barry Desmond (minister for health at the time) says. 'Had the tragic remains of that baby been found today, the State would immediately have taken DNA, and it would have been preserved for any future inquiry.'[3]

- After several hours' consultation with their lawyers, the nuns at Ann Lovett's school had agreed to a filmed statement for RTÉ. 'It is difficult to find words to express how the staff feels on this sad and tragic occasion,' read the head nun from the prepared statement. 'We have gone through the past week with Ann's family and have shared their grief and their sense of loss. Ann was an intelligent and bright girl who took an active part in school activities and was interested in her studies. She seemed happy in school and gave no indication of being under stress. No one on the staff knew that she was pregnant. Had we known about Ann's pregnancy, we would have taken her with understanding and compassion, as would be normal practice. We would have helped her to accept it, to cope with it, and also put her in touch with those who could enable her to make the necessary arrangements for the proper care of herself and of her baby. We respect and

---

3   *The Irish Times*, 5 May 2018.

accept the personality and individuality of each of our pupils. The circumstances of this tragedy reflect an element of mystery on everyone's part.'[4]

Shot in the school, the filmed clip shows a roomful of female teachers in woolly jumpers grouped silently and obediently around the principal, Sister Maria Plunkett, in full black regalia. By a fluke of fate, the zoom function on the cameraman's equipment had stuck, so the whole of the nun's message is read in the same static, wide shot, underlining the rigidity of the response, the inflexibility of the wording, the enforced groupthink – only one teacher absented herself from the choreographed farce.[5]

Ann Lovett was a clever, bright girl. Presumably she knew only too well 'the necessary arrangements' and 'compassion and understanding' traditionally offered to pregnant, unmarried girls in Ireland. Particularly young girls who felt they had to kill themselves rather than reveal the father's identity. Maybe it was a form of 'compassion and understanding' she gambled she could do without?

Irish Examiner journalist Conall Ó Fátharta, who has worked tirelessly to expose abuses within Mother and Baby Homes, including illegal adoptions, vaccine trials and 79 per

---

4   Boland, Rosita, 'Ann Lovett: Death of a "strong, kick-ass girl"', *The Irish Times*, 24 March 2018, https://www.irishtimes.com/life-and-style/people/ann-lovett-death-of-a-strong-kick-ass-girl-1.3429792.

5   *SCANNAL*, 27 December 2004.

cent death rates, found that, in 1967 Ireland, over 97 per cent of mothers with babies 'born outside wedlock' were forced to give up their babies for adoption by the Church or by their families then still under the thumb of the Church. As Ava Stapleton wrote in TheJournal.ie on 24 August 2018:

> Unless you were rich or had influence, you did what you were brainwashed into doing back then. People who blame the families for the Church's crimes and State collusion have no idea what they are talking about.

In a report by the HSE, the government health executive, quoted by Ó Fátharta, stated that 'unmarried mothers were considered little more than a commodity for trade amongst religious orders'.

Understanding and compassion indeed.

A letter issued by the diocesan secretary to the Catholic primate, Cardinal Tomás Ó Fiaich, deemed it 'rather unfortunate' that Ann Lovett did not 'make it known even to her friends who might have been able to help her or did not seek medical assistance independently of her parents or teachers', and went on to say: 'Why she chose to keep her secret will never be known', finishing with 'her sad death reflects more on her immaturity than on any lack of Christian charity amongst the family and people with whom she lived'.[6]

---

6   *The Irish Times*, 27 December 2014.

Talk about blaming the victim!

Young people at the time were in an impossible position. There was no sex education. All of the schools were run by religious orders where sex education was forbidden; the general approach was to tell us nothing: what we didn't know we wouldn't try. Contraception was only legally available for married couples and only on prescription from a GP. Even condoms could be bought only on prescription.

Girls interviewed at the time said they 'wouldn't like' to use contraception; it made them seem 'too calculating' and they were told by the nuns that if they did get pregnant, and if they did keep their babies, they would go to hell. As one girl said, 'My parents would have preferred me to drink or use drugs – you can hide those but you can't hide a baby.'[7]

One of the very few official voices raised on Ann's behalf was that of Nuala Fennell, founding sister of the Women's Movement and then minister of state with responsibility for women's affairs and family law. She called the deaths a 'national tragedy' and pushed for an inquiry, 'regardless of whose sensibilities were hurt'.[8] No inquiry was ever held.

A priest, sent in to replace the one who had so clearly known what was happening outside his window that terrible evening, spoke on television some years later: 'Nobody

<hr>

7   Lentin, Ronit, 'Death that Shocked Ireland', *The Age*, 1 June 1984, https://news.google.com/newspapers?id=jhoRAAAAIBAJ&sjid=-5JQDAAAAIBAJ&pg=4787%2C146122.

8   *The Irish Times*, 24 March 2018.

knew. Not one single person knew.' He said the silence of the people of Granard was all the media's fault. The media 'arrived like enemies, like police for a criminal.'[9] The priest said the media were 'intrusive', an intrusiveness 'bordering on uncaring barbarity'.[10]

The Irish media that supposedly descended on Granard 'like locusts' consisted mostly of female reporters from Dublin – from RTÉ, *The Irish Times*, *The Irish Press*, the (then *Cork*) *Examiner*, Emily O'Reilly, Nell McCafferty, Ronit Lentin, Lorelei Harris.

Hardly barbarians.

Yes, Nuala Fennell likened the town to 'the valley of the squinting windows', but it was the town's self-imposed *omertà* that showed more starkly than a thousand gladly given interviews the loneliness and rejection Ann Lovett must have faced.

Nothing to see here. Move along now please. Repressed, hypocritical, *vicious* Ireland at its very worst.

On 5 May 2018 a chink of light was allowed in when a senior journalist with *The Irish Times*, Rosita Boland, published an in-depth interview with Ann Lovett's boyfriend, Ricky McDonnell.

In a ghastly Irish version of Romeo and Juliet, he

---

9   *SCANNAL*, 27 December 2004.
10 Boland, Rosita, 'Ann Lovett: Death at the Grotto', 31 January 2004, https://www.irishtimes.com/news/ann-lovett-death-at-the-grotto-1.1304620.

described how he, then sixteen, and the fourteen-year-old Ann, had had a sexual relationship for months, until her fifteenth birthday when she arrived at his door late, 'sobbing and crying', her thighs 'bruised and scuffed'. Had she been raped? 'She just cried. She begged me not to tell anybody. Not to say anything.' After that evening she 'pushed him away'.

Several days after Ann's terrible death, her mother invited two of her friends to go up to her room and choose a memento. The girls found two letters and remembered these words jumping out: 'If I'm not dead by 31st January I'm going to kill myself anyway.' And, 'People will be better off when this happens.'

The second letter was for Ricky. The girls brought it to his house. In it, Ann said she loved him, how sorry she was, and that the reason 'she was going to do it, was that nobody would believe I [Ricky] was the father of that child'.

Within hours the local priest had arrived at the house. He read the letter, then ordered McDonnell to burn it: 'It'll destroy the town.' McDonnell, confused and grief-stricken, allowed the letter to be burned and was then taken by the priest to the gardaí, where he reported the assault/rape Ann had told him about the previous April. He was not questioned about it, nor was he given a copy of his statement. The next day the priest brought him to the bishop. The bishop demanded to know everything he had told the police and then swore him to silence 'on the seal of St Peter', holding out his bishop's ring to be kissed. McDonnell was then taken on a three-day trip by the priest to get him out of town; on his return, he was offered a room and odd jobs work at the priest's house. A couple of months later the priest arranged a visit to the then minister for justice and McDonnell was recruited into the army.

Job done.

The Mafia was leaving nothing to chance.

Three months after Ann's death, her sister, Patricia (14), committed suicide. At the inquest into the death of her second daughter, the mother gave the following information: she had gone to bed at midnight. Her husband had come to bed at 3 a.m. and woken her later to say 'Patricia is crying'. Patricia was pronounced dead from an overdose at 5 a.m. At the inquest, which Diarmuid Lovett couldn't attend as he'd had a heart attack, the pathologist said there was 'a bruise on the left side of her chin and an abrasion on her left cheek'.[11]

To this day the truth has not come out.

Weirdly, up to 2018 and Rosita Boland's *Irish Times* piece, no photograph of Ann Lovett, not a single one, existed in the public domain; memorably in May, in grainy black and white, a young girl stared out from the front page of *The Irish Times*: thoughtful, hurt, angry, utterly alone Ann.

Oh *Ireland*.

---

11   *The Irish Times*, 5 May 2018.

LASHING BACK

Before and after the rise and fall of the Irish Women's Liberation Movement, the Church's opposition to women's rights had been unceasing, and with the Church still having more or less total control over 'ordinary' lives and over our political leaders, its writ held.

With hindsight, perhaps we should have seen that a backlash to the fight for equality was inevitable; looking back, it was tragic that the Women's Movement was so reduced and scattered, that a concerted fight back didn't, couldn't, happen.

In 1971 Archbishop McQuaid was still saying things such as: 'to speak of a right to contraception is to speak of a right that cannot even exist'.[1] Acknowledgement of the new reality was incredibly slow to come. Still, throughout the 1970s and 1980s, starting with a Supreme Court ruling in 1973 stating there was a constitutional right for 'married couples to privacy, which included a right to contraception', legislation for the liberalisation of contraception began to trickle onto the statute books.

It was enough of a trickle to alarm right-wing Catholics; they believed these liberalisations were highly dangerous. Abortion would be next. And so, in the 1980s, a small

---

1   *The Irish Times*, 24 March 2018.

band of ultra-orthodox Catholics came together: PLAC, SPUC, the Congress of Catholic Secondary School Parents' Associations, the Irish Catholic Doctors' Guild, the Guild of Catholic Nurses, the Guild of Catholic Pharmacists, the Catholic Young Men's Society, the St Thomas More Society, the National Association of the Ovulation Method, the Council of Social Concern, the Irish Responsible Society, the St Joseph's Young Priests Society, and the Christian Brothers Schools Parents' Federation. Their lobby was so powerful they managed to browbeat three separate political administrations into compliance, and in 1983 a campaign to insert the infamous 'Eighth Amendment', giving a foetus equal rights to life as that of the mother, into the Irish Constitution began.

The referendum to insert the Eighth involved a brutal, bruising fight – and it was one the right-wing Catholics ultimately won.

Of course the stated aim of the anti-abortionists – 'banning abortion in Ireland for ever' – did not, could not, stop abortions; it just exported the 'problem' to England. It was hypocritical from day one. Let the women go abroad. We'll carry on with the pretence of virginal whiteness here at home. This in a country where you couldn't even buy a bloody condom.

In a ferocious piece, 'Caoineadh Mná na hÉireann', in *The Best of Nell*, McCafferty wrote after the amendment had been carried:

We women failed ourselves. We conducted a debate on male defined terms and we lost the debate. It has been shattering and ugly and we have been forced onto our knees. For the moment let us mourn.[2]

For women here, 'the Eighth' was to have appalling consequences.

Just six months after the Eighth Amendment referendum had been carried, ushering in a massive chill factor concerning everything to do with contraception and abortion, Ann Lovett died, and, three months later, another 'pregnant outside of marriage' young woman, Joanne Hayes, was flayed on hypocrisy's altar. She was a single mother who'd kept the baby she had had with a married man, got pregnant again by the same man and gave birth to a stillborn, second baby in a field on her family's farm, where she buried it. The gardaí, almost exploding out of their uniforms with righteous indignation, arrested her for yet another dead baby found on a beach seventy-six kilometres away, trying, and almost succeeding, in sticking both baby deaths onto her, citing 'superfecundation', or the simultaneous birth of two babies by two different fathers.

She was treated so brutally by the gardaí, their manipulation of evidence was so extreme, that a tribunal of inquiry

2   McCafferty, Nell, *The Best of Nell: A Selection of Writings over 14 Years* (Cork University Press, Cork, 2005), p. 62.

was set up. Far from examining the police attempts to frame her and her family, a panel of male 'experts', lawyers and medics descended from Dublin and put the young mother through weeks of cross-examination, forensically discussing the dilation of her vagina at the birth of her first child, where and when she had had sex with her married lover, whether she loved her lover or just loved 'what men were prepared to do with her'.[3]

The wise men of professional Ireland gathered and asked this slip of a girl 2,000-plus questions. She collapsed repeatedly. She was revived so the questioning could continue, so sedated, according to Nell McCafferty's account in *The Kerry Babies*, that her head was bobbing off the court microphone.

It was nine months since the referendum to ban abortion had been carried, three months since Ann Lovett's death – was it perhaps the first time that all of those people who had screamed themselves blue in the face about being 'pro-life', pro-babies, pro-foetuses, had second thoughts? That they realised creating an environment so hostile to young pregnant women that they and their babies died was not perhaps what we all wanted?

Hundreds of women all over the country certainly believed so. They sent single yellow roses wrapped in cellophane,

---

3   McCafferty, Nell, *A Woman to Blame: The Kerry Babies Case* (Cork University Press, Cork, 2010), p. 161.

wrapped in love and solidarity to Joanne Hayes, c/o the Tralee courtroom where the 'trial' was taking place.

Very strangely, in the final paragraph of his summation of his report into the 'Kerry Babies case', Judge Kevin Lynch (now dead), who had conducted the tribunal on grounds that it was as if the Hayes family were suing the gardaí for damages, something the Hayes family never even attempted, concluded:

> The Law Officers in the Office of the Director of Public Prosecutions were correct in their decision that the charges [against Joanne Hayes] should be dropped. The principle underlying this decision is correctly set forth by Mr. Donal Browne, the State Solicitor for County Kerry, when he said that it would not be right to put a citizen to the ordeal of a Trial when there clearly was not the evidence to justify the prosecution.
>
> Dated the 3rd day of October, 1985.[4]

The whole thing was an obscene sham.

---

4   https://ptfs-oireachtas.s3.amazonaws.com/DriveH/AWData/Library3/Library2/DL035878.pdf.

'CRACKPOTS' AND 'THE EIGHTH'

Despite the horror of Ann Lovett's death, and of what Joanne Hayes was so publicly put through, the conjoined twins of Catholic Church and State lumbered on.

In a television debate on the evening the referendum to insert the Eighth Amendment was carried, its architect, barrister William Binchy, said that a few 'crackpots' might challenge it but essentially the legislation was 'sound'.

Oh, how wrong could you be?

One of the Eighth Amendment's first public horror stories arose in 1992, when a suicidal fourteen-year-old girl, pregnant as a result of rape, was taken to London by her parents for a termination. Her parents asked the gardaí if DNA from the foetus could be taken and used in evidence. The gardaí immediately informed the attorney general, who issued an injunction, forcing the girl and her parents to come home. Five days later, a justice of the High Court heard the case. Ten days later he ruled that despite the rape, the age of the victim, despite her being suicidal, she had good loving parents and so the pregnancy must go ahead. Five days later again, an appeal was lodged. The following month the Supreme Court ruled that the termination, in England, could go ahead. The child miscarried two days later in a London hospital.

The misery and trauma of those weeks for the child, and for her parents, can only be imagined. You would think the inhumanity of the imbroglio would have had every lawyer and doctor in the country out demanding that the Eighth Amendment be repealed.

Sadly not a bit of it.

The then archbishop of Dublin, Desmond Connell, said, 'I have deep reservations about the re-affirmation by the courts of the notion that there are circumstances where abortion is medically justifiable.'[1]

Fair enough, you might say; if this is what the man believes he's entitled to that belief. But hang on a minute, isn't this the same archbishop who resigned after the Murphy Report and a television documentary entitled *Cardinal Secrets* revealed he had been 'economical with the truth' about the sexual activities of priests in his diocese? After the report by Judge Yvonne Murphy, which deemed the Dublin archdiocese's preoccupations in dealing with cases of child sexual abuse to be:

- the maintenance of secrecy,
- the avoidance of scandal,
- the protection of the reputation of the Church, and
- the preservation of its assets.

---

1   *The Irish Times*, 29 November 1997.

All other considerations, including the welfare of children and justice for victims, were subordinated to these priorities. The Archdiocese did not implement its own canon law rules and did its best to avoid any application of the law of the State.[2]

These were the same 'men of God' who said we couldn't so much as touch each other without going to hell FOR ALL ETERNITY and this archbishop still believed that a fourteen-year-old child victim of rape could not have her pregnancy terminated?

Oh please, fuck *off.*

---

2   Report by Commission of Investigation into Catholic Archdiocese of Dublin, 2009: http://www.bishop-accountability.org/reports/2009_11_26_Murphy_Report/.

THE BISHOP, THE AMERICAN GIRL
AND THE BABY

One of the biggest cracks in the 'empire' came with the revelation that Ireland's favourite high-flying bishop, Eamonn Casey, the all-singing, all-dancing, all-good-living bish, was actually the father of a seventeen-year-old boy whose mother, in her early twenties and recovering from a miscarriage and a divorce, had been sent by her father from America to his friend and relative in Ireland, the bishop. So tender was the bish's care that he seduced the beautiful young American, had a passionate affair with her, panicked like hell when she told him she was pregnant, desperately tried to force her to get rid of the baby, get it adopted, MAKE IT GO AWAY, and, when she wouldn't, packed her and the baby, their baby, back off to Amerikay.

Lovely.

A bishop, a prince of the Church, a man dressed in purple silk, was fucking a woman young enough to be his daughter! A bishop now had a big strapping lad with the same woman! The same bishop had refused to recognise his big strapping lad, though he did send irregular subventions from the Church coffers! It was only when the American mom, Annie Murphy, outed the bish for not even acknowledging his son's existence, never mind supporting him despite years of desperate pleas, that the story broke.

Hundreds of thousands of women (and men) stopped believing in the Church overnight, their heads in flitters with the cognitive dissonance of it all.

And that was only the start of the avalanche.

Further collapse in previous 'blind' faith came with RTÉ producer Mary Raftery's documentary series *States of Fear*, aired in April 1999. This showed how the Catholic Church-run institutions – the industrial schools and the reformatories – were rife with the sexual and emotional brutalisation of young Irish children. Beatings, semi-starvation, insufficient clothing, filthy living conditions, overwork, emotional abuse and sexual assault were rife. Further horrors were revealed with the publication of her book *Suffer Little Children*, and another television documentary, *Cardinal Sins*, detailing further clerical sexual abuse cover-ups.

All these institutions had been supported financially by the State, which, over the decades, had turned a blind eye. Let the Church, let the nuns, let the brothers get on with it.

The Church's response? Cover your asses – sorry, assets – at all costs.

In 1993, after the nuns of the Sisters of Our Lady of Charity sold a property that had been a Magdalene Laundry to a developer, a 'mass grave' was found. One hundred and fifty-five women's bodies were uncovered. Many of the women were found with plaster casts still on – on ankles, wrists, arms. One was found with no head. Only seventy-five had death certificates, many had no names other than the religious monikers doled out by the nuns, such as 'Magdalen of Lourdes' or 'Magdalen of St Cecilia'.[1]

Responding to queries from Mary Raftery, a nun in charge, Sister Ann Marie Ryan, said coolly that the exhumation and re-interring of the bodies of the women 'was approved by all relevant authorities, and we have had no queries from families about our decision in the intervening time'. In truth, the bodies had been cremated by the nuns, ensuring traceability would never be an option.

The nuns pocketed IR£63 million for the site; the women who'd slaved for them were burned.[2]

Brides of Christ indeed.

---

1   *The Ragged Wagon*, 3 February 2013, https://theraggedwagon.word-press.com/2013/02/.
2   *The New Statesman*, 17 July 2013.

LETHAL PERIL

In my own life, my marriage was in lethal peril. By the time our babies arrived – my daughter Chupi in 1984 and my son Luke in 1987 – I had let too much slip. Glossed over too many glaring no-nos. I had never 'strayed' again, or certainly didn't tell him if I did, while his 'strays' had become ever more blatant. At this point I was certain 'my' man was now seriously involved with someone I knew and had trusted, and it devastated me.

The artifice began to crumble: I wasn't Miss Jolly Hockey Sticks any more; I was a frightened girl without her carapace, alone and responsible for two tiny people. And the truth had to be faced: I wasn't being jealous/paranoid/mad. He *was* having it off with someone else. However, when I tried to dig the truth out, I was laughed at, told I was imagining things. Even my family were largely unsupportive and I was told I was being paranoid.

After one of his frequent trips to London, when I was informed by a friend that he had spent the night at the other woman's place, he arrived home in Ireland the next day in a lather: it was all a terrible mistake. He had nowhere else to sleep. It meant NOTHING! Etcetera, etcetera.

And so it went on: backwards, forwards, sideways. He said. She said.

About five largely uneventful months slipped by and then he announced that he had to travel to Africa for work. Several days later, a friend from London sent a postcard. He'd been at a dinner party. Such a fun evening! My man was there. The life and soul! Actually he'd never seen him in such good form!

I finally got the courage to pull the plug on the whole sorry fandango.

Not ending up in the loony bin during this period was definitely a struggle. After years of denial, after years of saying I was mad for even thinking something was 'going on', my ex was now living with his new woman full-time. That it was someone I was once close to only added to my feelings of betrayal. Such incandescent rage flooded through me that madness seemed uncomfortably close.

I knew I was definitely damaged. Damaged long ago by Mum's retreat into profound depression, by Dad's retreat into profound unhappiness, by nobody talking to anyone. Damaged by boarding school. Damaged by religion and the guilt nonsense rammed down our throats by nuns and priests from day one. Damaged by my ex and his new partner. Shock, shock, trauma and more shock, and none of it dealt with. I knew now that Armageddon had come and I was poorly equipped to deal with it.

Separated now, I was exhausted and there was so much shit to face. There was the shit that I was going to have to face the future alone as a 'deserted wife' with two tiny 'deserted' children. The shit that 'my' man was laughably not so; was quite happy, in fact, to pull the plug on his life with the babies and me. Oh he'd be sad for a day or two, he told me, but he'd get over it. The shit that my babies would have to face growing up without their dad. The shit that we were penniless now. The social welfare officer visited and promised two years of deserted wives' allowance. 'That should see you out,' he said. I rushed to the mirror after he left. Did I look so old, so fucked, that the social welfare officer thought I would be dead within two years? I was forty-two. *If I died, what about my babies?*

What about my babies? I cried into the night. What about them? answered the patriarchy. Here's £69 a week. Now fuck off. The patriarchy, which had designed marriage – insisted on it, 'to protect women and children' – didn't give a crap. 'Our' solicitor, weirdly energised when I went to visit, toddler at side, baby on knee, asked: 'So what's it going to take for you to fuck off? £30,000, £35,000?' I don't remember how I made it back down the stairs on my rubber legs.

At one point I was so desperate that I went to visit the local priest to beg £50 to get us into the next week. He slammed the drawer of his desk, stuffed to the brim with chequebooks, so hard that he caught his jacket sleeve; it ripped as he tried to lock the drawer and yank out the sleeve at the same time.

When I wailed to the barrister in her consulting rooms, she got up, eyeing me over her spectacles: 'We could try a mental health angle.' That shut me up.

My solicitor, a new and wonderful one, said he'd had word from 'the other side'; they wanted to engage in mediation. I smelt a rat. Why did hubby want to get into mediation? It wasn't his style at all. My solicitor said I should probably agree. Not agreeing might seem like obstinacy on my part.

This led to two middle-aged ladies in an oblong room, him directly in front of them, me to the side. He was in a new, very expensive cashmere and silk suit, while I was in charity shop duds. The middle-aged ladies – supposed mediators – were all over him like a rash. Yes! Of course! Absolutely! We couldn't agree more! Finally turning, sad-eyed, to me, asking: Why didn't I agree to him having the children at Christmas, Easter and for the summer holidays? It would be lovely for them. Wouldn't it? Yes, all right, he was living with someone who wasn't their mother, but children are very *adaptable* you know, Rosita.

Adaptable! Oh how I hated those middle-aged hand-maidens to the patriarchy.

Still, by that point I was so not a feminist that it was a joke. I was too exhausted, too poor and too lacking in self-belief to make some grand gesture like, Fuck You All I'm off to Narnia, while taking a baby under each arm and making a new home and a new life on the Aran Islands.

It was the early 1990s by this point, and there was still no divorce in Ireland. Legal separation was as good as it got, and that was a costly and complicated nightmare. Oh yes,

I certainly began to understand feminism backwards, when I was a 'deserted wife', i.e. a total failure in the eyes of the patriarchy. In the eyes of the world.

I had no money. My self-esteem (hahaha! what's that?) was down the toilet. I also felt that my family were letting me down – nobody seemed to understand what I was going through, to want to visit or help in any way. I was especially upset by my mother's seemingly uncritical acceptance of what my husband and his new amour had done. The children and I became totally isolated.

After ten months of much-advertised, champagne-fuelled bliss, my ex and his new squeeze split when it turned out that he was having an affair with yet another lady, in yet another country. Cue much wailing and lamentation on the part of the newly deserted; I failed to dredge up even the slightest sympathy.

It was exhausting being angry, but, deep down, part of me figured if I stayed that way at least I wouldn't get depressed. I'd seen so many 'deserted wives' slide, terrifyingly quickly, into depression. One walked out into traffic in London. One let her children be taken by the father and then drank herself to death. Many, many of us grabbed another man, no matter how much of a loser he was, how much of a drain, as anything was better than being alone, rejected, 'deserted'.

If I keep fighting, I thought, I'll keep sane. If I stay away from the dreaded pharmaceuticals – the SSRIs and the Prozac and the Valium – and stay well away from the loony bin, I figured, I'll be psychologically battered and bruised, but my mind will still be my own. I'll fight through.

Still, grief's horrible pathways demanded to be travelled: shock, denial, anger, bargaining, acceptance. I almost got permanently stuck on anger.

It was so UNFAIR!

I went on and on and on about love, but all I did was hate. I hated myself. I hated my situation. I hated Mum. I hated my family. I hated our house. I hated our poverty. I hated our kitchen. I hated that we were never properly warm, the central heating off for months at a time. I hated our fridge with its poverty-stricken contents. When the children were in bed I drank cheap red wine and hated some more. I was deep into post-traumatic stress and didn't even know it.

To be fair, it was pretty stressful. The children and I had gone from money, two cars, well-stocked fridge, crates of wine, regular and costly home improvements, weekly grass cutting and garden maintenance, trips abroad, nights out, straight to penury, to absolutely not a fucking penny. All of which wasn't of course the hardest part; the hardest part was the betrayal.

Still, slowly, slowly, survival began to feel, and look, a bit more like life. After years of tramping through courts in Wicklow, Dublin and finally London, I got a small alimony for us, and my feminism redeveloped so far as kneeling in front of the hi-fi speakers at night, when the children were asleep, listening to Gloria Gaynor's 'I Will Survive'.

Slowly, slowly, as the children got bigger and stronger, they began to deconstruct my post-traumatic stress-disordered self and put a kinder, more human self back together.

I began to pick up my old books: *The Female Eunuch*, *The Second Sex*, *Our Bodies Our Selves*, *Women and Madness*, *Sisterhood is Powerful*. A wonderful friend and editor, Anne Harris, gave me a job writing features and doing a radio review column in one of the Sunday papers.

One summer's day an artist friend thrust an original copy of *Chains or Change* into my hand: 'for you'. Feminism's old words fell heavy as chains on a stone floor inside my heart. I was that 'deserted wife'. I desperately needed to do something. For my children. And for me.

GETTING CLEAR

Two things forced change: one was that my daughter's health crashed.

My darling daughter. Actually all three of us had had weirdly crappy health for years, despite the fact that we had been living high up in the Wicklow mountains with apparently clean air, wide-open spaces, fresh water straight off the mountain, tobogganing in the fields in the snowy winters, swimming in the river and lakes during the summers, walking, and playing badminton using a net we rigged up in the front garden.

When my daughter was ten she was lying on the sofa after yet another bout of flu followed by yet another round of antibiotics. At the time every apparent 'cold' or 'flu' for either child ended up as bronchitis; twice ending with pneumonia with my son. I suddenly thought: this is insane, all of these antibiotics are going to destroy their immune systems. I'm going to take them out of school, see if we can manage at home.

That's how we began home schooling.

Home schooling has a bit of a dodgy name these days thanks to zealous right-wing practitioners in the US keeping their kids at home so that they can proselytise them better, but in the 1960s it had been part of the 'revolution':

natural birth – home birth if possible – breast feeding, living in harmony with nature, treating children as the vibrant little beings that they are, eager for learning from day one. We'd done home birth so why not try home schooling? By the early 1990s, sadly, home schooling had dwindled to a tiny cohort of mostly rural-based families. Still, it had some pretty impressive advocates, including one of the leaders of our revolution here in Ireland, Patrick Pearse, who summed up his attitude to schools in his *The Murder Machine*; Ivan Illich, who brought his brilliant mind to bear on the subject with his 1971 book *Deschooling Society*; and the redoubtable Maura Mullarney and her husband Brian, who home schooled their eleven children in a tiny cottage up a mountain boreen in Co. Wicklow. Maura described their successes in her book *Anything School Can Do You Can Do Better*.

In the beginning, of course – with Chupi ten years old and Luke seven – it was fairly chaotic. Freed from the restrictions of a timetable, we did a lot of messing, ate a lot, found a million excuses (me) to go to the local shopping centre, panicked (me) when we looked like hillbillies in the same shopping centre and began frantic searches for (cheap) clothes that would make us look like everyone else – searches that usually ended in frustration and tears.

Frustration and tears also attended a lot of writing and reading sessions with my son. Why could he not get it? I employed all my old Montessori-learned tricks, to no avail.

Still he avidly consumed audiobooks, graphic novels and history. One of the great delights of bringing up the little people is you get to revisit parts of your own childhood you had at the time only half understood. While my daughter happily employed herself doing maths and reading Jane Austen, my son devoured anything to do with history, the house filling up with audiobooks on Alexander the Great, the Patrick O'Brian seafaring novels, George Orwell's *Homage to Catalonia* and, of course, all of Terry Pratchett – 'he's the best, Mum'. It was much, much later that we discovered he was dyslexic.

Reactions to my decision to home school were not always favourable. A local priest, back on holidays from a stint in Africa, came to visit. For the entire length of his visit our solid-fuel cooker belched dense black smoke. After five minutes I could barely make him out across the table. He began with some pleading for me to bring the children back to school, but soon there was very red-eyed weeping. I thought it was the smoke until I realised he was really crying. In Africa, raising the host one morning, he said, he realised he didn't believe. He laughed nervously, thick anthracite smoke swirling around his head. 'Nothing.'

I made him tea. Gave him smokes. Thumped him on the back. Home schooling arguments were dropped.

Next the local sergeant came to visit. His large uniformed presence filled the kitchen. 'You know now, Rosita, it's against the law to take the children out of school?' Thanks to home-schooling friends nearby – our mainstay throughout the home-schooling years – I knew it wasn't and had a battered copy of *Bunreacht na hÉireann* to prove it. Frowning, the sergeant skimmed the text of Article 42:

> The State acknowledges that the primary and natural educator of the child is the Family and guarantees to respect the inalienable right and duty of parents to provide, according to their means, for the religious and moral, intellectual, physical and social education of their children.

'And,' I pointed out helpfully, 'see this one here Mr Policeman' and read the third clause of Article 42 in a loud voice:

> The State shall not oblige parents in violation of their conscience and lawful preference to send their children to schools established by the State, or to any particular type of school designated by the State.

That last bit is a lie; properly intimidated, I hadn't pointed out anything. But Mr Plod put down my battered pale-green copy of the constitution, picked his cap up off the counter, muttered, 'I'll be back', and was gone.

'Was that true, Mum?' asked my son, referring to Article 42.

'It is,' I said, 'look,' I went, 'it's here, we could read it', holding out the page, but his interest was already returning to the huge Lego tropical landscape he was building across the kitchen floor.

A year into the 'experiment' one of my extended family members wrote a long letter, saying taking a child out of school was akin to murdering them. Wasn't that a bit extreme? There followed stilted conversations at family get-togethers: 'Still involved in that bloody awful home-schooling nonsense, Rosita?'

Every home-schooling family has their own way of going about things. We did a mixture of structured – get the damn books out and get some bookwork done – followed by unstructured – okay we're going to Inishboffin next week, right? Mostly, it was a bit of both – books in the morning, Glendalough, Inishboffin, or Connemara whenever we could.

Ironically, it was when I tried too hard that the home schooling backfired. Usually because it was something I had always wanted to do and had never been given, or subsequently given myself, time to explore. Take art. I borrowed hundreds of books from the library: *How to Paint with Watercolours*, *How to Draw Horses*, *Painting with Oils for Teenagers*, all of which gathered dust, and library fines, until, pouting, I brought them back. 'Mum,' my daughter said one afternoon, 'if I want to do a painting I'll just do it, there's no need to get more books from the library.' There and then she did a painting of our wonderful cat, Vanilla, looking characteristically cranky and majestic, sitting beside an ornate pepper grinder from Rome, both cat and grinder captured in their absolute essence. After that I left the library books out of it.

In public, I was defiant. In private, I agonised.

In the meantime, we recorded some memorable highs: reading aloud the whole unabridged version, including poems and songs, of *The Lord of the Rings*; starting in the mornings in bed, with cups of 'bed tea', out in the garden during the day, finishing by the fire in the evenings. Eating breakfast outside, cooked by my son over a roughly made fire pit in the garden. Visiting the tiny local circus, spotting the sword swallower leaving later, swords neatly tucked under a sleeping baby in a large pram. Whamming down huge frozen fields on a toboggan the children had made, throwing yourself off just before hitting the massive stone wall at the bottom. Cheering wildly when my daughter got first prize in *The Beano* art competition. Glowing with pride when a visiting Oxford alumnus had a two-hour in-depth conversation with my by-then-just-teenage daughter regarding the mores and politics of the Jane Austen oeuvre, the Oxford lady coming to me afterwards, 'You do realise how brilliant she is, don't you?' Unrestrained celebrations when my son, as a young teen, suddenly began reading. Kicking off with Bram Stoker's *The Snake's Pass*, he was not to be stopped until he'd consumed all of the classics. Looking on, awestruck, as my daughter designed and made, with her brother's help, two skating ramps (in-line skating was that winter's craze). Helping out, awestruck again, as my daughter decided – at the instigation of fashion editor, and super-loyal friend, the wonderful Deirdre McQuillan – that she and her brother should write a cookbook, gathering together all of the recipes for the wheat-free, sugar-free, MSG-free, dairy-free cooking we were now committed to, and ultimately seeing their cookbook, *What To Eat When You Can't Eat Anything*, born at our kitchen table. Out of print now here, it's still selling steadily in America.

The year my daughter was eligible to sit her Junior Certificate, we were in an Eason bookshop in Dublin. She drifted over to the schoolbooks section and came back with a selection. 'I think I could do this Mum.' We bought all the books on the Junior Cert course there and then, and nine months later were driving across the country to a little boarding school, the only one at the time willing and registered to take home-schooled students for State exams. My daughter had a streaming cold, swollen glands, a pounding head and was chalk white with nerves going into a small school where everyone knew everyone, but was resolutely determined: she was going to do it. When the results came in three months later she'd aced it.

Next she decided she wanted to go to boarding school, like her favourite cousins, for her final two-year cycle. I was terrified, and proud. Terrified for her health, while so proud that she wanted to make this leap on her own. She was offered places, and a scholarship, in three schools, but after two weeks was forced to come home with glands the size of courgettes, a roaring fever and a racing heartbeat.

Things suddenly came to a head. The doctors, who up to this point had dismissed my visits to the surgery as the actions of 'an over-anxious single parent' – one of them actually wrote that in the referral letter to the consultant – began to take things seriously. Something must be wrong if my daughter couldn't continue boarding school.

My daughter was diagnosed with 'bronchiectasis'. I, that over-anxious single parent, instantly and totally blamed myself. My darling daughter climbed onto the sofa and didn't get off it for a year. I spent the time frantic and crying.

Everyone, as they always do when ill health strikes, had their own solutions: you should take her out more. It's probably psychosomatic. Send her back to school. Toughen her up. Coming back from a frantic whizz to the shops with my son one evening I saw my daughter walking down the lane to meet us; she was like a flickering flame, barely, barely there.

I thought I would lose my mind with fear.

It wasn't until we left the mountains, a couple of years later, that my children's health finally improved.

MUM

And then the second thing that forced change: Mum died.

For years my relationship with Mum had been grim to ghastly. I could not understand, or forgive, why she didn't seem to support the children and me after the separation. I could not forgive her for not only ignoring the trauma of the events that deprived the children of their dad and sank us into poverty, but also the denial that what happened had been so cruel, so awful, so traumatic that it had driven me to the edge of madness. On one Mother's Day I fantasised about arriving at her house dressed as a guerrilla fighter – in full fatigues, toting a machine gun, belts of ammunition slung shoulder to hip each side.

Now what do you say, Mommie dearest?

Praise the Lord, and pass the ammunition as the old American folk song goes, a few weeks before she died Mum wrote to me and apologised. I was deliriously happy.

After that, we visited, wrote and rang every day. For the week of Mum's dying and death I was with her every day.

Everything that was good in Mum came to the fore that last week. Death was standing at her garden gate, blowing on his fingernails, and Mum was saying how I must go home and get the children their favourite supper. We had five days to fall back in love with each other. By the time Mum died

I felt healed, understood. Loved. I think Mum did too. To lose Mum, having just re-found her, was horrendous, but to have lived on with the legacy of a poisoned mother–daughter relationship forever would have been unbearable.

It was 2001. The beginning of the new.

IRELAND OLD, IRELAND NEW

Throughout the 1990s and 2000s, the Eighth Amendment continued to wreak havoc on the lives of Irish women.

In 2010 Michelle Harte, a mother of one who was receiving cancer treatment, became 'unintentionally' pregnant. The hospital advised termination but the hospital 'ethics' board refused it. The 'threat to the mother's life' was not substantial enough. Cancer treatment was stopped. By the time she got money, plane tickets, passport, Michelle Harte had to be carried onto the plane to London. With treatment so peremptorily halted, the cancer returned with a vengeance. Just months later she was dead.

But it was 2012 and the terrible death of a beautiful young Indian dentist, who had presented to a hospital in Galway clearly miscarrying her much-wanted first child, that was to highlight the cruel insanity of Ireland's abortion laws. Savita Halappanavar, medically trained, knew just what was happening and begged day after day for a termination. Her waters had broken, her foetus had no chance of survival, her body was trying to miscarry, but still the hospital refused an abortion because of a foetal heartbeat. A midwife told Savita, 'We don't do that here, dear. It's a Catholic thing.'[1]

---

1   *The Irish Times*, 9 April 2013.

Savita developed sepsis, delivering a dead foetus as the hospital was setting up an IV line. Fatally ill, she died, her hands and feet black with sepsis, two days later.

Thanks to a tip-off to an *Irish Times* journalist, Savita's story was made public. Tens of thousands of women, and men, took to the streets. Never again. Never again. NEVER AGAIN! shouted the posters.

It was the start of the fight back.

The government meantime voted down two separate Repeal and Fatal Foetal Abnormality Bills, describing activists calls for change as 'shrill' and likely to alienate 'middle Ireland'.

In 2013 came the first March for Choice. Savita's death symbolised what all women faced as long as the Eighth Amendment remained, as long as the life of the foetus was legally on a par with the life of the mother. Her death became world news thanks to *Irish Times* journalist Kitty Holland, daughter of journalists Mary Holland and Eamonn Mc-Cann. But how many Irish women had suffered and died in, or out of, our maternity hospitals without anyone knowing?

What we do know is that ten to twelve women have travelled to the UK from Ireland every day to have an abortion for years now. They have had to do this in secret, usually in a frantic rush to get money, organise childminding, buy plane tickets, secure accommodation and journey to the UK and back, travelling home without medical supervision, either before or after their operations.

As if Savita's terrible death wasn't enough, two years later the consequences of the Eighth Amendment being in place were once again demonstrated in the case of Miss P, a young pregnant mother with a fatal brain injury. She was kept artificially 'alive' because she was pregnant, and because there was a foetal heartbeat, though her seventeen-week-old foetus had no chance of survival. Her brain and her body were disintegrating, the nurses slathering on make-up so her tiny visiting children wouldn't be terrified at the sight of her. Her grieving parents were begging the High Court to have life support turned off, but the seven doctors in charge, so frightened of the law, were unable to let her, and her foetus, die with dignity.

Something had to give. Something was beginning to give. In 2016 a deeply conservative and Catholic Taoiseach, Enda Kenny, set up the 'Citizens Assembly' to look at the Eighth Amendment and make recommendations for the future. At the time a lot of people thought it was a cynical kicking-the-can-down-the-road exercise, but actually it turned out to be rather clever. Thank you, Enda.

As the fight back against Ireland's draconian abortion laws suddenly gathered momentum, the fight for same-sex marriage and to end discrimination against gay and lesbian couples simultaneously moved forwards and backwards, through commissions, committees, High Court hearings, etc. It was driven by the articulate Marriage Equality group, which simply asked: why shouldn't same-sex couples have the same rights and protections that the marriage legislation gave to heterosexual couples? Their campaign, and its success, was a huge breakthrough, showed just how radically Ireland was changing, and resulted in the referendum on same-sex marriage being passed in 2015 with a whopping 62 per cent YES.

As the first country in the world to enact equal-marriage laws via a public vote, Ireland rushed into the history books and out onto the streets.

The success of the same-sex marriage referendum gave hope to many women now gathering to fight for the legalisation of abortion. Could it be that Ireland was evolving? That the thousands of young, and many not so young, who had flown home to vote in the same-sex referendum – many of whom had been forced to emigrate by the economic crash of 2009 – were making damn sure Ireland was going to be a better place for all? That they could get their voices heard and create a new, happier, inclusive Ireland? Could it?

Yes, it seemed it could.

Veterans from the 1983 abortion battle, like Ailbhe Smyth, joined forces with other pro-Repeal groups and formed 'Together for Yes', an umbrella group made up of over seventy organisations, led by the National Women's Council, the Coalition to Repeal the Eighth Amendment and the Abortion Rights Campaign.

Naturally the battle for free, safe, legal abortion was going to be inherently more difficult, more divisive and more painful, than the battle for same-sex marriage. The same-sex marriage referendum was an occasion for rainbow-coloured joy over the whole country: for gay couples, for those who believed in liberty, and for thousands of parents who'd seen their own gay children going through hell to gladly now come out to vote big fat YESs to support them. But abortion? Firstly it was often still so secret and shameful, so *not* discussed between one generation and the next, that just bringing it into the open was going to be painful.

Secondly the weight of years of the Catholic Church's propaganda, stating 'human life must be respected and protected absolutely from the moment of conception. From the first moment of his existence, a human being must be recognised as having the rights of a person – among which is the inviolable right of every innocent being to life' had been dinned into everyone for so long that changing hearts and minds was going to be a job.[2]

In 2016 we saw the establishment of Enda Kenny's 'Citizens Assembly', with ninety-nine 'ordinary' citizens invited to discuss the Eighth Amendment, to discuss abortion. Experts were invited in and listened to. Everyone, even those grandstanding for their constituency back home, was listened to. For the first time as a nation we started thinking, and talking, about abortion, rationally. And, crucially, from a woman's point of view.

---

2   The Catechism of the Catholic Church.

To everyone's surprise the Citizens' Assembly over-whelmingly recommended abortion without restriction for up to twelve weeks. Crikey, we really were evolving. And the twelve weeks was a recognition of reality: thousands of women were already buying abortion pills on the Internet, taking them without supervision at home in the first weeks of pregnancy.

Following the Citizens Assembly decision, a government commission was set up inside parliament. Again the experts were called in. Again, despite some blowhards threatening the usual fire and brimstone, walkouts, moral collapse of the entire nation, etc., the experts and, crucially, the women were listened to.

A date for a referendum was set.

In the final weeks, our new young Taoiseach declared for the referendum and, with a few glitches, the entire front bench, led by the minister for health, also declared for it, go-ing out to canvass support, and of course have their pictures taken with the grassroots workers who'd been slogging away at this for decades. But they were at least there.

It was thrilling.

It was also frightening. Canvassers for Yes were spat at, punched, called murderers, threatened with abortion themselves. Right-wing Catholic American money and right-wing American students poured in to tell us all what to do. Hideous, bus-sized posters showing abortions in graphic detail were set up around Dublin. When Facebook and Google announced they were no longer allowing pages – for either side of the debate – to be put up, the No side went crazy. What about freedom of speech? Rather rich from the people with links to ultra-nationalist organisations, who adamantly refuse to divulge where their apparently bottomless funds come from.

Meanwhile the personal stories that poured out during the referendum campaign were what really changed things. These were our mothers, sisters, aunts, daughters – our friends. 'Ordinary' Irish women. Women with dying babies inside them forced to travel to the UK for terminations. Women whose babies had no skulls, no brains. Women carrying foetuses without kidneys. With multiple sets of chromosomes. Women carrying babies who had no chance of life. None. All of them forced to travel to Liverpool or London for terminations in strange hospitals, bleeding in taxis and in train stations on the way home. Their babies' remains delivered by courier weeks later, or brought home in a cardboard box.

Despite the huge response to the Yes campaign, fear was still so pervasive. The day of the vote I had lunch with my children and their partners. The sun was shining. We were at an outside table of a local wine bar, everything was picture-perfect brilliant, but still there was fear. Would the referendum pass? Would it be struck down? Would we have to go back to the No Ireland the antis were so keen on? My son, ever the optimist, said even if it doesn't pass, it will never be so bad again.

When the exit poll results came through at 10.30 p.m. that night, it was explosive. We'd won! 66.4 per cent YES to 33.6 per cent NO. Things would never, ever, EVER, be so bad again!

The next morning the sun shone on Ireland. Women couldn't stop smiling at each other. A mural of Savita Halappanavar painted on hoardings the day before on Dublin's hipster corner, beside The Bernard Shaw pub, became a sort of impromptu shrine, tearful women scrawling their messages: *My Vote was for You. So Sorry Savita. We are Very Sad for Your Family. This Vote was for You. Here in Ireland that Loves You Savita. Never Again.*

Walking home along the canal, it felt as if a huge weight had been lifted. That the dead hand of the Church, of patriarchy and conservatism, had finally been lifted. That women in Ireland were finally equal. Our bodies our own.

What a day.

***

Still, as if to remind us all of what we were campaigning for, what we were fighting against, in the midst of the liberalisations came the horrific revelations from the Tuam Mother and Baby Home in early 2017.

Old Ireland rearing its ugliest head.

Revelations of these horrors first came to light in 2014, after years of research by an amateur, local historian, Catherine Corless. She detailed the discovery of the remains of almost 800 babies, 'wrapped in cloth and stacked like Cidona bottles' according to one local, thrown into old cesspits or septic tanks, in secret, in the dead of night, via a secret passage from the home's chapel, by the Bon Secours nuns who then ran the 'Mother and Baby' Home in Tuam, Co. Galway.

The Daily Mail, in a piece published in June 2014, referenced a 1944 local health board inspection of the home, which 'reveals the conditions the children and their mothers lived in'. It showed that in April that year, 271 children were listed as living there with sixty-one single mothers, a total of 333 – way over its capacity of 243. One thirteen-month-old boy was described as a 'miserable, emaciated child with voracious appetite and no control over bodily functions and probably mentally defective'. In the same room was a 'delicate' ten-month-old baby who was a 'child of itinerants', while one five-year-old child was described as having 'hands growing near shoulders'. Another thirty-one infants in the same room were described as 'poor babies, emaciated and not thriving'. The majority were aged between three weeks and thirteen months and were 'fragile, pot-bellied and emaciated'.[3]

In a piece for the *Independent* on 8 June 2014, Caroline Crawford wrote:

> Death records obtained by local historian, Catherine Corless, for the home make clear the sheer level of neglect prevailing

---

3   *Daily Mail*, 2 June 2014.

throughout the institution. A list of the children who died shows that in many cases infants were dying within days of being born. In one outbreak of measles, twenty-seven children died together. Others died from fits, oedema, abscess of the scalp and in one case, laryngitis.

If the reports had been about baby and child misery and death rates in a concentration camp they could hardly have been more horrific.

In 'causes of death' recorded in another notoriously hideous Mother and Baby Home in Bessborough, Co. Cork, journalist Conall Ó Fátharta noted the following: marasmus (severe malnutrition), congenital debility, gastroenteritis, spina bifida, congenital syphilis, pneumonia, bronchitis, congenital heart [defects], congenital deformity, tubercular peritonitis, cardiac shock, heat stroke, mastoiditis, tonsillitis, prematurity, meningitis, tubercular meningitis, cerebral meningitis, congestion of the lungs, abscess of the bowel and convulsions, 'among others'.[4]

How twisted the nuns' own female nature must have been to have overseen the viciousness that was part and parcel of these 'homes'; the punishments, shamings, barbarous treatment, all flowing from the Church's 'teachings' on 'fallen women' and their 'illegitimate' babies; it was a barbarity that held up until very recent days.

4   *Irish Examiner*, 9 November 2015.

Very recent days indeed.

In an interview with TheJournal.ie on 7 March 2017, a councillor, Deirdre Wadding, remembers being induced ('for social reasons' written on her medical records), giving birth alone and on a bare metal table, aged eighteen, in a room in the convent. There were no antenatal visits. No doctors. No midwife. She haemorrhaged heavily after her induced baby had been delivered by forceps and suction, and lay alone in the room for three days. She saw her baby for the first and last time on the fourth day, when he was being taken away for adoption:

> I think it was the whole sense of you're a pariah, you're a pariah and somehow being punished for the crime of being a normal, natural, sexual human being. So we were punished for a crime that didn't exist and that punishment was a life sentence – it was having your child taken away.

This was Ireland.

This *is* Ireland. In a mini documentary by Al Jazeera in 2019, solicitor for survivors of Tuam Kevin O'Higgins believes 'Church and State in this country are still wedded in a poisonous pact', meaning no real justice will come for the Tuam Babies. Katherine Zappone, the minister for children, supported the government in refusing full exhumation, full DNA testing, full post-mortems. As the reporter for Al Jazeera said, 'Survivors think the government would rather bury the truth than dig up the past', going on to note:

> There are dozens and dozens of places like this (Tuam) around Ireland. A full investigation into what happened at all the Mother and Baby homes would be explosive and could destroy the reputation of the Church.[5]

It's a measure of the Church's continuing stranglehold on politics here that, despite an international wave of horror at the revelations from Tuam, then from Bessborough, the airwaves here alight with the stories of women in their sixties, seventies, eighties, their voices cracking with emotion as they remembered their days in these terrible Golgothas, the government is still stalling on tackling the Church head on.

Survivors of the 'homes' still cannot get full birth records. Adoptees cannot get full records. The exhumation of the 800 little baby bodies at Tuam, announced with great brouhaha by the government in October 2018, will now take place, but there will be no post-mortems conducted to work out why the little ones died. Not one.

The €1.3 billion of redress due from the Catholic Church to victims here remains mostly unpaid.

Meanwhile, the orders of nuns and priests, brothers and sisters who run the institutions that perpetrated this abuse,

---

5   Aljazeera.com, 19 September 2019.

with assets worth hundreds of millions of euros, are still giving the run-around to attempts by successive governments to make them pay even paltry recompense. The pope, who sits on assets worth billions, the Vatican's wealth rated at between $400 and $800 billion, its affairs so secretive no one is sure of the exact amount, this apparently kind-hearted guy who rules over a Church that has abused hundreds of thousands of women and men and children worldwide, many of them in Ireland, has done little to nothing but support the fighting off of claims by victims through the courts.

To date only 14 per cent of the money initially pledged by the Church has been handed over to the Irish government. The Bon Secours order – which was in charge at Tuam, which buried those babies in septic tanks – is by no means defunct, a relic of our dark past; instead, it is currently the largest provider of private healthcare in Ireland, with hospitals in Cork, Dublin, Galway, Tralee and Limerick. It employs over 3,000 people, including 450 medical consultants.

In 2017 the journalist Shane Phelan revealed that the Bon Secours order had been paid €43.5 million, over the previous ten years, for leases on buildings and interest on loans. Just for leases and interest on *loans*.[6]

Let's not beat around the bush here: the Catholic Church is loaded.

And not to forget there was, and is, abuse elsewhere.

6   *Irish Independent*, 11 March 2017.

In a piece for the *Irish Examiner* in 2012, writer Victoria White called out the hypocrisy of blaming 'Mammy Church' for everything when the 219 children buried in unmarked graves in Protestant institutions like the Bethany Home in Rathgar cry out, unheeded, for justice.

But here, in Ireland, it is the Catholic Church that has had top-dog position for so long and so must take the major portion of blame.

And must pay for its crimes.

HOW FEMINISM ALMOST DIED

Now that feminism is aflame again, it's frightening to think how it almost withered away during the 'boom' years. You were a killjoy, a 'feminazi', if you cared about politics, civil rights, feminism. Neoliberalism, capitalism's slickest and most slithery offspring, ruled. Deregulation, 'letting the market find its own level', 'a rising tide lifts all boats', and other such nonsenses were the mantras of the day. Kicked off by Ronald Reagan in America and Margaret Thatcher in the UK, ultra capitalism was born. There was the 'revolution of the rich', followed by the rise of the 'super rich', the rise of mega corporations hundreds of times bigger and richer than national governments, hundreds of times more powerful.

Between 1979 and 2006 the income of the richest 1 per cent rose by 256 per cent.

Feminism wasn't immune. The old 'sexual politics' was to be swapped for a 'focus on self-transformation'; a feminism re-packaged as 'pink power', or endless, apparently limitless, and largely idiotic, let's be fair, consumption.

Second-wave feminism's project to interrogate capi-talism was shelved in favour of girls becoming 'laddettes', 'consuming porn', watching footie, being down with the boys. Prostitution and pornography, once seen as the ulti-mate degradation of women by the patriarchy, mirroring the generalised subjugation and exploitation of women within the patriarchy, were 'fun' things everyone could enjoy.

At an address to the Australian Labour Movement, Maureen Mathews, a member of the 'Eros Foundation', a lobby group for the sex industry founded in 1992, and a young woman speaking as a 'feminist representative for the sex industry', advocated that 'women can, and indeed must, fuck their way to social freedom and justice'.[1]

The patriarchy was no doubt delighted with her.

While we're on the subject of sexual politics, a word, or two, here about pornography.

Oh dear God, pornography.

As Kate Millett so poignantly said about the struggle for sexual liberation: 'We got pornography when what we wanted was eroticism.'[2]

First defined in *A Dictionary of Medical Science* in 1857 as 'a description of prostitutes or of prostitution', pornographic material was initially mostly confined to brothels.[3]

Hard to believe these days when it's as ubiquitous as fast food. And even more poisonous.

Initially the Women's Movement and pornography

---

1   Stark, Christine and Whisnant, Rebecca, *Not for Sale: Feminists Resisting Prostitution and Pornography* (Spinifex Press, Melbourne, 2004), p. 207.

2   Cooper, Emmanuel, *The Sexual Perspective: Homosexuality and Art in the Last 100 Years in the West* (Psychology Press, Hove, 1994), p. 207.

3   https://www.psychologytoday.com/ie/blog/sex-wars/201903/what-does-porn-mean-anyway.

might have been seen to have some common objectives – liberating the body, specifically women's bodies, and sexuality, from the cold dead hand of puritanism. Tragically, and to all of our costs – female and male, but most of all to us females – while the Women's Movement fought to retrieve women's bodies from patriarchy's rules and restrictions, the pornography 'industry', with the brutal implacability of capitalism, spotted an open market, transforming what was once the purview of dirty old men in dirty old raincoats into a multi-billion dollar 'business' that every year becomes more violent and more misogynistic. It now invades every aspect of modern western culture, creating what feminist campaigner against pornography Gail Dines calls 'the pornification of culture', or the 'hyper sexualisation of culture', with films, fashion shoots, pop stars treading as close to the line between 'hard' and 'soft' porn imagery as they dare. The now $12 billion dollar porn 'industry' pours an endless stream of hard-core porn, or the subjugation, humiliation and rape of women, into laptops, phones, tablets and desktops, and from them into the minds of men, mostly men, including many 'men' as young as ten years old, around the globe.

Of course what porn offers is a lie. As one brave commentator on *The Guardian*'s website, in response to a Julie Bindel piece, wrote in 2014, 'I'm a male consumer of porn and I think the overwhelming majority of it is vile. It's like wanting a drink and the only choice is meths, paint-stripper or windscreen wiper fluid.'

Still, if you can get the majority of men addicted, wiper fluid will do just fine.

At the birthing of neoliberalism, when Margaret Thatcher's dictum 'There is no such thing as society' was taking hold, and regulations were being quietly removed from the banks and the speculators, it became quite hip to say it was okay for women and girls to 'consume' pornography, to say everything in the pornography parlour is quite okay, that 'sex workers' can individually 'empower' themselves within the prostitute/john transaction etcetera, et-bloody-cetera.

Perhaps the apex of such bullshit was reached in 2011 with the publication of *Fifty Shades of Grey*, the porn tale that went on to become a film of the same name, grossing $600 million worldwide, with Hollywood slathering on the glitter and the gloss and the super-sleek interiors to 'sex up' porn's usual hideous tripe: men dominating women for men's sexual gratification.

Thousands upon thousands of women bought into the hype. Like turkeys being brainwashed into thinking Christmas and Thanksgiving are holidays designed just for them, they swallowed the PR bullshit: *Fifty Shades*, we were croonily reassured, was a 'Romantic Story for the Porn Age.'

A few brave feminists stood against the tide, chief among them Gail Dines, professor of sociology and women's studies at Wheelock College, Boston, who wrote in her 2015 review of the film in *Feminist Current*: 'This was not just a movie about sexual violence, but a film that depicted, in unbearable detail, how to lure a lonely, isolated child into "consenting" to sexual abuse.'[4]

Yup, that's what was lapped up – child abuse, or woman-as-child abuse, in sensational interiors.

And these issues are not academic. Just a fortnight before Christmas 2018 in England, in *England,* the cradle of democracy and fair play, a multi-millionaire property developer in his forties, who'd left his pregnant wife and two children to hook up with a twenty-six-year-old mum of one, was given a three-year sentence for her brutal killing. He was charged with manslaughter only, because the crown prosecution feared a murder verdict wouldn't stick and the man would walk free. His legal defence was simple: she 'liked' 'rough sex', or, as one commentator sarcastically dubbed it, 'the Fifty Shades of Grey' defence.

The case caused outrage in the UK. Labour MP Harriet Harman called for a formal review, questioning why the prosecution did not proceed with a murder charge. 'We cannot have a situation where men kill women and blame them,' it was said. 'No man will ever be accused of murder again if he can always say, "… she wanted it", she will never be able to say, "no I didn't" because he's killed her and therefore she hasn't got a voice.'[5]

---

4   https://www.feministcurrent.com/2015/02/18/review-watching-50-shades-of-grey-is-torture/.

5   *Marie Claire*, 21 December 2018, https://www.marieclaire.com.au/john-broadhurst-natalie-connolly-death.

After a day partying with 'her' man, the young woman, mother of a ten-year-old girl, bled to death after she suffered forty separate wounds, including severe damage to her vagina and internal organs, a busted eye socket, head wounds and face wounds. She also had a household cleaner repeatedly sprayed in her face. Then her 'lover' went up to bed and slept till morning, at which time he rang emergency services assuring them his girlie was 'dead as a doughnut'.

His barrister assured the court that when his client left the dying young woman and went upstairs to beddy byes he was certain she would be okay; they had had 'drunken sex' in the same location, the bottom of the stairs, the week before and she'd been in 'the same position' and had been fine.

The 'Fifty Shades' defence worked brilliantly. Clearly this very pretty young mum had been 'asking for it'. Asking for her vagina to be ripped asunder, her eyes smashed out of their sockets, her head busted open, her pretty face sprayed with 'bathroom cleaning product', i.e. bleach, asking to be left to die, to bleed to death, naked except for her skirt rolled up around her waist, while he slept the sleep of the (un)just upstairs.

They were in love, said the man's barrister. The case was about 'negligence', about somebody 'losing a loved one'.[6]

Dear God.

---

6   BBCNews.com, 17 December 2018, https://www.bbc.com/news/uk-england-46591150.

Modern pornography is *about* eroticising violence against women. A modern standard porn image involves one girl/woman with three men orally, anally and vaginally raping her while she's shouted at, spat at, abused, cum splattered on her face. Porn sites, readily available on the web and titled 'Anally Raped Whores' and 'Gag Me then Fuck Me', indicate the level of violence involved. Women working in the porn industry are indeed routinely wrecked by brutal sex, leading to prolapsed anuses, torn vaginas, STDs, not to mention shattered selfhoods. As one sex worker told Dines, it takes years to recover.

Here is Dines again:

> For those of you who think that radical feminists exaggerate or cherry-pick the worst of the porn industry, I have an experiment for you. Type 'porn' into Google and click around the most well-travelled websites that appear. With mind-numbing repetition you will see gagging, slapping, verbal abuse, hair-pulling, pounding anal sex, women smeared in semen, sore anuses and vaginas, distended mouths, and more exhausted, depleted and shell-shocked women than you can count. You will not see two people having sex; you will see images depicting a level of physical cruelty that would not be out of place in an Amnesty International campaign.[7]

---

7   https://overland.org.au/previous-issues/issue-207/feature-gail-dines-sharon-smith/.

There's also an effect on men – porn is now the gateway to sex education for most boys, often starting as young as ten – as can be seen in the increasing levels of violence against women all over the world. Here is Gail Dines again:

> To assume that porn is mere fantasy and does not impact on the way men think and feel is to ignore decades of research on how images frame our social construction of reality. Porn is an industry, and like other industries it shapes the way we live. The fashion industry shapes the way we dress, the food industry the way we eat, and the sex industry the way we think and have sex. To argue otherwise would be to make the ridiculous claim that the only industry that has no power in the real world is porn.[8]

In the infamous Belfast Rape Trial of 2018, where three young rugby players boasted about 'roasting' and 'pumping' a nineteen-year-old girl who left their house bleeding, the scenes described could have been lifted straight from a porn film. The young men were acquitted of rape, though their careers were in tatters, and thousands upon thousands of women, and men, north and south, took to social media to support the young woman. 'I Believe Her' became the most used hashtag of the year.

The weird thing is that an 'industry' that is predicated on misogyny, rape, violence, drugs, coercion, disease and

---

8   *Ibid.*

trafficking, and which is run by, and for, one section of humanity (men) at the expense of another (women), gets to call itself an industry and is not called out as a criminal enterprise. It is an indication of how far we still have to travel to gain equality between the sexes.

Flip it around for a minute and imagine a world in which teenage boys and young men were kidnapped, drugged and trafficked by women. Then filmed being brutally raped (snuffed if necessary), screamed at, spat at, abused, again by women, *solely for the sexual gratification of other women*. Don't you think the guys might get a tad upset? If we spewed our 'films' into every handset, desktop, laptop, smartphone and tablet on the planet? Set up our own $600 billion dollar 'industry' from which we made millions on the back, literally, of one half of the human race for the gratification of the other?

Second-wave feminists believed pornography was the scene of a crime – a crime against women. They were right. They still are.

Dervla Murphy, one of the finest and bravest women on this planet, who has travelled hundreds of thousands of miles alone in some of the wildest parts of the world, said recently she would be terrified if her three young granddaughters now headed off on similar trips, that pornography on tap has turned the world into a viciously dangerous place for women.

How horribly sad is that?

In 2017 Professor Gail Dines helpfully put together a few statistics (italics mine):

- Women perform 66 per cent of the world's work, produce 50 per cent of the world's food, and earn 10 per cent of the world's income. *Ten per cent.*

- Women own 1 per cent of the world's property. *One fucking per cent!*

- Women comprise 70 per cent of the world's poor. *Seventy per cent!*

- Ninety per cent of the world's billionaires are male.[9]

Women 'fucking their way to the top' is apparently harder than you might think.

Still, in recent years – particularly since the 'bust' – a great many people have woken up. Capitalism's illusions have once again been torched. Politics, and feminism, are suddenly back on the agenda. It was as if the sticky plastic goo of boom promises abruptly fell away and there we all were, the party over, the cheap drink drunk, the brutal hangover kicking in.

So many people were affected:

– You were young, you were married, you had kids, you were in a house in the arsehole of nowhere that you had paid hundreds of thousands for, you and your husband's jobs were going going gone, childcare was ruinous and your house, which had turned out to be a gimcrack confection of

---

9   Dines, Gail, 'Neoliberalism and Defanging Feminism', lecture, https://www.youtube.com/watch?v=kDcTt0emXhE.

zero insulation, subsiding walls and shoddy everything, was now worth a fifth of what you'd paid for it, and anyway your chances of paying for it were nil.

Lovely.

– You were young, you were married, you had kids, you were in an apartment with rents even higher than during the boom times with leaking walls, crappy furniture and no possibility – none! – of saving up for a deposit for a house since all of your joint incomes went on rent and childminding while the housing market, now taken over by politicians and vulture funds, climbed ever higher to another bubble/bust.

Fabulous.

– You were young, you had as yet no kids, you had a job and you had an apartment. Sadly the rents on apartments had now skyrocketed to such levels – thanks to the aforementioned banks and vulture funds – that saving for a house was out of the question. You were a Millennial. The first generation in a long while in the western world likely to be less well off than their parents.

Smashing.

– You were middle-aged, like a good boy/good girl you'd saved for years and years and years with the banks so that you and your family could live comfortably through the later years. Overnight the banks went poof! and all your savings – hundreds and hundreds of dollars/pounds/euros – went poof! too; after months of trying to fight the banks, fight the government with absolutely no response from anyone, ever, you went out into your garage one night and hanged yourself. It was too much.

Oh dear.

– You were elderly, young, middle-aged; you looked on in amazement as the chief architects of the 'biggest bank bust in history' received risible sentences for perpetrating a €7.2 billion fraud via Anglo Irish Bank; CEO David Drumm, Willie McAteer, John Bowe and Denis Casey getting six and a half years to two and a half years behind bars with a 25 per cent reduction for good behaviour. Within months all four had been transferred to Loughan House, an open prison in Cavan where prisoners have 'a very relaxed regime', can come and go as they wish, receive visitors, and get day/weekend releases. At the same time the leading political cheerleaders for the 'boom', Bertie Ahern and Brian Cowen, were receiving annual pensions of over €150,000 each.

Right.

– You were a woman, you saw the new government coming in promising a new broom, a new transparency. Within a handful of years you saw the old horrors returning, with repossessed houses sold to foreign vulture funds, the aptly named multinationals who swooped in to feast on the carcasses of people's dreams in an Ireland busily fanning the flames of yet another property 'boom', and an Ireland where homelessness has reached epidemic proportions, as the banks, the politicians, the vulture funds, the landlords once again make a killing.

– You were a human being and you watched in horror as migrants fleeing torture, environmental catastrophe, social collapse, drowned in the sea or died inside trucks. You listened in shock to Lucia Bird, senior analyst at the Global Initiative Against Transnational Organised Crime on RTÉ's *The Business* on 29 October 2019 say that 40 million people have been trafficked into 'forced labour', i.e. slavery, in today's world in a 'business' now worth $10 billion.

– You were a feminist and you looked at the world and you thought does it have to be like this? Is it always going to be like this? Or is the whole thing a massive patriarchal disaster?

– You are feminist again, and you know that something needs to change. You need to act.

IN THE END

In the end – and in the beginning and in the middle – feminism is not about hating men, it's not about women becoming men, and it's not about women asserting power over men. I'm with Simone de Beauvoir here: to make things better we have to come together, 'to carry off this supreme victory – a future where women and men are equals – men and women must unequivocally affirm their brotherhood'. And, eh, sisterhood, Simone?

Feminism is not about blaming men, nor about pushing a few women to the top so they can be 'she-men' for the patriarchy. Feminism is about deconstructing patriarchy; radical feminism is about replacing patriarchy entirely. Feminism is about creating a world fit for everyone. Not just for the few. As Professor Gail Dines wrote:

> As feminists, we know that we 'still can't have it all', but this is not simply because of brutal workplace schedules. Helping a few women reach positions of power so they can get rich and hang out with the boys was never a goal of progressive feminism. Our goal should be to restructure institutions from the inside out, and for this we need women – and, indeed, some men – who bring feminist politics to our economic, political, and social organisations. We are not naïve: these women and

the changes they bring won't be welcomed with open arms by male-dominated institutions. But change they must, if all women are to enjoy real economic, legal and political equality.[1]

Ah the patriarchy! A world where a few psychopathic alpha males club and claw their way to the top and proceed, via their henchmen and henchwomen, to make life hell for everybody else.

Where the world's precious resources are crammed into the hands of fewer and fewer alphas so that Mother Nature can be raped more efficiently, more disastrously, more comprehensively – all of course in the name of 'business' and 'progress'. Where war, drugs, pesticides and the 'sex trade' are the most profitable businesses on our tiny planet. Where the property markets of virtually every city on earth are now in the hands of politicians, billionaires, lawyers and vulture funds. Where in Ireland, a tiny country off the west coast of Europe with a tiny population, and after the biggest bank bust in history, political leaders are gifted pensions of around €3,000 a week while over 10,000 people, including families with children, have been made homeless thanks to a financial regime that has so recently, and so clearly, been shown to be catastrophic for so many.

A world where America has installed as the 'Leader of the Free World' a misogynistic bully with a bad attitude, a

---

1   *The Guardian*, 25 June 2012.

very strange relationship with his daughter, a history of links with the Mafia, an apparent love of the KKK, fascists and the alt-right, not to mention a weird hairdo.

A world where, according to UNICEF, an estimated 25,000 children a day die of hunger, and that's not counting the little ones who die in wars, the little brown and black ones … who gives a damn about them? Who's even counting how many of them are blown to smithereens by gleaming machines shown off in arms 'fairs', big fancy get-togethers where the psychopaths send their henchmen to buy the latest, deadliest technology to blow the fuck out of other humans.

A world where, according to an *RTÉ News* report on 15 February 2019, more babies than soldiers died in wars around the world in the past five years. More *babies*.

A world where brute force is valued over everyone and everything. Where the carpet-bombing of women and children – and their men – in defenceless enclaves is tacitly accepted by men in suits back home as 'collateral damage'. Where 80 per cent of the victims of today's wars are civilians. Eighty per cent. 'Oh go on, push that drone button, Josh. Who gives a shite if an entire wedding party in the foothills of the Hindu Kush is wiped out? They're all fuckin' terrorists as far as we're concerned buddy!'

Marilyn French, wonderful, lifelong feminist and author of *The Women's Room* – it sold twenty million copies and was translated into twenty languages – said in Vanessa Engle's

BBC documentary *Women* that she was 'fed up' with a patriarchy where the men went off to war, killing each other 'and a great many of us', while women were left holding the babies, dead and alive. 'I'm sick of it. I always have been.'[2]

At its core, feminism is saying: surely we can do better than this? Surely we can at least imagine a world where the basics are taken care of? Where parents and their children are supported over bombs and guns. Where people have homes. Where people can afford decent food. Where there is clean water. Where there is education. Where there is safety from the threat of war. Where women are no longer routinely raped and/or killed and/or trafficked into prostitution. Where the overweening ambitions of so-called alpha males are kept in check by a society that values equality and decency.

A world where we can all – women and men, young and old, gay and straight, binary and non-binary, black and brown and yellow and pink and white, big and little, fat and skinny – make a new beginning.

Unless the alphas succeed in killing off all of us, plus every living thing on the planet, feminism will keep coming back. Like spring bulbs pushing up through the sodden earth, hello, *hello*! If it almost died off during the boom, these days it's more robust than ever.

Deborah Frances-White, author of *The Guilty Feminist*

---

2   *Women*, BBC Four, first aired March 2010. Directed by Vanessa Engle.

and host of the eponymous podcast, believes things are happening so fast that fifth-wave feminism is already upon us, incorporating all the work of our wonderful foremothers, plus the work of the second wavers of the 1960s and 1970s who laid bare the politics of the patriarchy, through to the very recent third wave, when 'intersectionality' and the realities of being 'queer', black, broke, not able-bodied, trans, not binary, were, *had to be*, integrated, if feminism wasn't to become just another part of the patriarchy.

On to fourth-wave feminism and the explosion of the fight onto social media, which was fuelled by the wonderful Laura Bateman and her hugely successful site 'Everyday Sexism', and the MeToo and Time's Up movements' exponential expansion.

Started by civil rights activist and sexual assault survivor Tarana Burke in 2006 in New York, the MeToo movement went international in October 2017 when actress Alyssa Milano co-opted the tag and sent out her now-famous tweet asking women who'd been sexually harassed to answer her with the hashtag MeToo. Within a fortnight MeToo had been re-tweeted 500,000 times. Fourth-wave feminism was born.

Bodily autonomy was everything for these fourth wavers. Any ambiguity about rape was *over*. Whatever we wear, wherever we go, yes means yes and no means no. These were the women who poured onto the streets after the election of Donald Trump, the women, and men, who poured onto the streets after the Belfast Rape Trial, all those who continued, and continue, the battle on Twitter and Facebook.

And now the fifth wave has arrived, says Frances-White, and it's all about action: 'Feminism can't exist in principle, it needs the oxygen of action' – on the street, in university campuses, in parliaments, in shopping malls. We have to stop treating feminism 'like our dying grandmother' and get her out there in the square yelling her head off.

'We've had ten thousand years of exclusion,' says this very un-guilty feminist, 'and we're going to bust that all down in less than a hundred? Oh *please*.'

Fifth wave is also about inclusion. 'Inclusion is a watchword of the second decade of the twenty-first century and its recent waves of feminism. But it's nothing new. Inclusion is the foundation of society. Inclusion is the reason human beings are at the top of the food chain'. But most of all fifthwave feminism is about maintaining a vocal and massive social media presence, which involves 'turning hashtags into consequences'. The ultimate hope is that the fifth wave will be 'a global army that crowd funds and realises proper, permanent changes can be made with the right strategies'. [3]

For the dream of equality to become reality we have to co-operate – straight, trans, bi, queer, black, working class, middle class, young and old.

---

3   Frances-White, Deborah, *The Guilty Feminist* (Virago, London, 2018), p. 10.

As lifelong activist Margaret Prescod said, at the end of the fascinating 2018 Netflix documentary *Feminists, What Were They Thinking?*, 'We'd better find our way to each other. We *need* each other because we are all on this planet and we are all in trouble right now.'

FEMINISM BACKWARDS

It was my daughter who urged me to go back and write about feminism. 'It's your story, Mum. *Own* it.' Like all super-disciplined creatives, I procrastinated for months. Don't want to. Can't. Who the hell wants to know about feminism any more anyway? Will not. Too busy! Shan't. *Non*!

When I eventually got going it felt like rowing out alone into the middle of a vast deserted lake. How to make a shape? What to say? Where to steer *for*? The whole enterprise seemed impossible.

Coming to shore now, I am so grateful that my darling daughter kept prodding me.

Leaving our mountain-based Wicklow home in 2004, battered jeep packed to the gunwales with teenagers, dogs, cats, books, clothes, paintings, possessions, the usual refugee grab bag, was unbelievably traumatic. As we turned out of our lane, our home in the rear-view mirror, I had to stifle a scream. Every blank window of the house threw out a desperate cry: you're leaving me here to *die*. It felt akin to abandoning one's best friend on the battlefield, but I drove on. We had to.

Within the year, the children's health had begun to improve. Chupi aced her exams at Sallynoggin College and was headhunted by TopShop before she could even complete her degree to take a slot in their brand-spanking-new store just opening on Stephen's Green. Luke completed his Leaving Cert, on his own, sitting by the stove in the beautiful Sandymount house we were renting; he then went to study film, first in St Kevin's College in Crumlin, and later in the national film school, IADT, in Dún Laoghaire.

These days, fifteen years since we left our Wicklow home, Chupi is a sensationally successful jewellery designer, specialising in gold pieces fashioned from nature – twigs, leaves, feathers and diamonds – her mountain past still in her present. Having dumped fast fashion and moved to 'shiny things', she now has her own business, *Chupi*, employing forty-eight people. *Forty-eight*! She married Brian, who is a very successful IT consultant, also with his own business. Luke also has his own successful business – a film production company, 'Little Beast' – and is engaged to beautiful Esme, also a filmmaker. He has become a wonderfully sensitive and creative director.

I am so proud of them.

Looking back on the time inside my marriage, I can see how I had been absolutely terrified of becoming a 'deserted wife', a 'lone parent'. It was definitely part of the reason I hung on for so long. And certainly the early, poverty-stricken years of lone parenting, plus grief, plus PTSD, were extremely painful and difficult. Most painful of all was that I was a lousy mother. Slowly, slowly, the ship turned around and the young ones began to thrive. I began to thrive. When I look back at the powerless creature I was inside that bad marriage I can only whoop with joy that I got out; that I got the children out with me.

Revisiting the past has been, as they say, a journey.

It's whizzed me backwards to childhood, to parents, to family, back to the 1960s and 1970s, to Gaj's restaurant and the birthing of the IWLM, and rushed me forward to the present, to 'Everyday Sexism', to MeToo, to 'I Believe Her', to the fifth wave, to feminism resurgent everywhere.

Feminism Backwards also whizzed me back to the Catholic Church; to the 'faith' I was brought up in; to examining the Church's shocking history of misogynistic bullying; to an Ireland where religious misogyny was in lockstep with the misogyny of the State – hence the ferocious outcomes: Mother and Baby Homes, industrial schools, Magdalene Laundries, censorship, puritanism, repression. And guilt, guilt, guilt.

How wonderful it is that we are finally getting clear.

It also rushed me back to my own terrible times, the times of marriage implosion, feeling let down by my family, and on to the brutal realities of 'lone parenting', of trying to parent when you're deep in post-traumatic stress.

Miraculously, in spite of the terrible times, my two wonderful children and I came through.

In reality, it was because of my two wonderful children that I came through. It was they who put me back together again. Showed me how to love.

Feminism Backwards also rushed me back to early

feminist times. To remember what we were fighting for, what we believed in, what became blaringly obvious the more we studied. As Mamo McDonald of the ICA (the Irish Countrywomen's Association) said, 'I wasn't born a feminist. Life made me one.'[1]

Feminism Backwards has remade a feminist of me, my feminist antennae removed, repolished and replaced. No longer a feminist in name and distant history, I feel I'm a feminist again in blazing reality. So here's 3,000 million bazillion cheers for feminism, the most wonderful and profound movement for social change there is – fighting for the liberation of women, fighting for the liberation of men, fighting for a better world for all.

My story. I hope I've owned it.

---

1   RTÉ Archive, *Hindsight*, 22 August 1994.

BIBLIOGRAPHY

Books

Bourke, Angela, *The Burning of Bridget Cleary: A True Story* (Penguin, London, 2001)

Bourke, Angela (ed.), *The Field Day Anthology of Irish Writing: Volume V, Irish Women's Writing and Tradition* (New York University Press, New York, 2002)

Ceplair, Larry, *The Public Years of Sarah and Angelina Grimké* (Columbia University Press, New York, 1991)

Cooper, Emmanuel, *The Sexual Perspective: Homosexuality and Art in the Last 100 Years in the West* (Psychology Press, Hove, 1994)

Chains or Change (Irish Women's Liberation Movement, Dublin, 1971)

Dinnage, Rosemary, *Annie Besant* (Penguin Books, London, 1986)

Ferriter, Diarmaid, *The Transformation of Ireland* (Profile Books, London, 2004)

Frances-White, Deborah, *The Guilty Feminist* (Virago, London, 2018)

Lensmen Photographic Archive, *The 1950s: Ireland in Pictures* (O'Brien Press, Dublin, 2013)

Levine, June, *Sisters: The Personal Story of an Irish Feminist* (Attic Press, Dublin, 2009)

McCafferty, Nell, *The Best of Nell: A Selection of Writings over 14 Years* (Cork University Press, Cork, 2005)

McCafferty, Nell, *A Woman to Blame: the Kerry Babies Case* (Cork University Press, Cork, 2010)

Meaney, Geraldine, *Sex and Nation: Women in Irish Culture and Politics* (Attic Press, University of Virginia, 1991)

Millett, Kate, *Sexual Politics* (Columbia University Press, New York, 2016)

Milotte, Mike, *Banished Babies: The Secret History of Ireland's Baby Export Business* (New Island, Dublin, 2012)

Morales, Maria (ed.), *Mill's, The Subjection of Women: Critical Essays* (Rowman & Littlefield, Maryland, 2005)

Redstockings, *Feminist Revolution: An Abridged Edition* (Random House, New York, 1978)

Richards, Maura, *Single Issue* (Poolbeg, Dublin, 1998)

Stark, Christine and Whisnant, Rebecca, *Not for Sale: Feminists Resisting Prostitution and Pornography* (Spinifex Press, Melbourne, 2004)

Stopper, Anne, *Monday at Gaj's: The Story of the Irish Women's Liberation Movement* (Liffey Press, Dublin, 2006)

Sweetman, Rosita, *Fathers Come First* (The Lilliput Press, Dublin, 2015)

Todd, Janet, *Mary Wollstonecraft: A Revolutionary Life* (Columbia University Press, New York, 2000)

Tóibín, Colm and Ferriter, Diarmaid, *The Irish Famine: A Documentary* (St Martin's Press, London, 2001)

Wollstonecraft, Mary, *The Vindications. The Rights of Men, The Rights of Woman*, ed. D. L. Macdonald and K. Scherf (Broadview Press, New York, 1997)

Articles

Brennan, Eoin, 'Television in Ireland: A History from the Mediated Centre' (ICA Conference, Japan, June 2016)

Grimes, Lorraine, '"They Go to England to Preserve their Secret": The Emigration and Assistance of the Irish Unmarried Mother in Britain 1926–1952', *Retrospectives*, Vol. 5, Issue 1 (Warwick University, Warwick, 2016)

Hartmann, Heidi I., 'The Unhappy Marriage of Marxism and Feminism', https://web.ics.purdue.edu Hartmann_1979

Horgan, Goretti, 'Changing Women's Lives in Ireland', *International Socialism* (Summer 2002), https://www.marxists.org/history/etol/newspape/isj2/2001/isj2-091/horgan.htm

Hunt Botting, Eileen, 'Making an American Feminist Icon: Mary Wollstonecraft's Reception in US Newspapers, 1800–1869', *History of Political Thought*, Vol. 34, No. 2 (April 2012)

Inglis, Tom, 'Origins and Legacies of Irish Prudery: Sexuality and Social Control in Modern Ireland', https://researchrepository.ucd.ie/handle/10197/5112

Mead, Rebecca, 'Postscript: Kate Millett's Radical Spirit', *The New Yorker*, 7 September 2017, https://www.newyorker.com/books/page-turner/postscript-kate-millets-radical-spirit

Ó hÓgartaigh, Margaret, 'Internal Tamponage, Hockey Parturition and Mixed Athletics', *History Ireland*, Issue 6, Vol. 15 (November–December 2007)

Robertson, Pat, 'Twenty Vile Quotes Against Women', https://valerietarico.com/2013/07/01/mysogynistquoteschurchfathers/

Smith, James M., 'The politics of sexual knowledge: the origins of Ireland's Containment Culture and the Carrigan Report (1931)', *Journal of the History of Sexuality* (1 April 2004), https://www2.bc.edu/james-smith-2/Politicsofsexualknowledge.pdf

Steiner-Scott, Liz, 'Female Activists: Irish Women and Change 1900–1960', *History Ireland*, Issue 2, Vol. 11 (Summer 2003)

Tóibín, Colm, 'Gay Byrne: Irish Life as Cabaret', *The Crane Bag*, Vol. 8, No. 2 (1984)

Newspapers/Magazines

Daily Mail
Evening Standard
Illustrated London News
Irish Examiner
Irish Independent
Marie Claire
The Avondhu
The Guardian
The Irish Press

The Irish Times
The New Statesman
The New Yorker
The Times (London)

Websites

http://gutenberg.net.au
https://irishhistorypodcast.ie
http://malcolmxfiles.blogspot.com
https://overland.org
https://theraggedwagon.wordpress.com
www.aljazeera.com
www.americanyawp.com
www.apnews.com
www.bbcnews.com
www.feministcurrent.com
www.fff.org
www.historyisaweapon.com
www.marxists.org
www.psychologytoday.com
www.rte.ie/radio1
www.thedailybeast.com
www.thejournal.ie
www.timeline.com
www.wikipedia.org

Documentaries

Hindsight, RTÉ Archive, 22 August 1994
SCANNAL, 'The Story of Ann Lovett', aired 27 September 2004
Women, BBC Four, first aired March 2010, directed by Vanessa Engle

Report

Report by Commission of Investigation into Catholic Archdiocese of
    Dublin, 2009

ACKNOWLEDGEMENTS

First, and always foremost, I would like to acknowledge my wonderful children – Chupi and Luke – who never stopped believing in me, and in *Feminism Backwards*. Annette Mc-Namee, who read the first drafts and urged: keep going, keep going. Eithne Tynan, who edited those first drafts with her usual brilliance and sensitivity. My darling coz Michele Sweetman, and Ursula Browne who held my hand as I leapt down the rabbit hole. Mary Feehan, managing director of Mercier, who responded to a tentative email with such positivity that I cheered inwardly for days. My editor, Noel O'Regan, who spent three months torturing me with requests for clarity and references. *Noel*! And to Wendy, who kept her nerve and her good humour at the eleventh hour when I lost mine.

Love and eternal gratefulness to all of the amazing Sisters who paved the way, some of whom are mentioned here: the Grimké sisters, Mary Wollstonecraft, Simone de Beauvoir, Betty Friedan, Angela Davis, Kathie Sarachild, Kate Millett, Sheila Rowbotham, Germaine Greer, as well as my wonderful co-founding sisters of the IWLM – Máirín de Burca, Máirín Johnston, Mary Maher, Nell McCafferty, Mary Kenny, Marie McMahon, Mary Sheerin, Moira Woods and Eimer Philbin Bowman, and dear departed sisters June Levine, Nuala Fennell, Mary Anderson, Mary Holland and Margaret Gaj.